Breed, Warren
The self-guiding society

THE SELF-GUIDING SOCIETY

WARREN BREED

THE SELF-GUIDING SOCIETY

Based on *The Active Society*, by Amitai Etzioni

THE FREE PRESS, *New York*

COLLIER-MACMILLAN LIMITED, *London*

A Division of The Macmillan Company

Printed in the United States of America

The Free Press
A Division of The Macmillan Company
866 Third Avenue, New York, New York 10022

Collier-Macmillan Canada Ltd., Toronto, Ontario

Library of Congress Catalog Card Number: 75–128472

printing number
1 2 3 4 5 6 7 8 9 10

PREFACE

Almost everybody wants justice and equality of opportunity. But how to achieve it? One thing certainly is required: Man must change his social institutions. But, almost everybody has a generous capacity to accept things as they are—or maybe to grumble some and carry on. Institutions are notable for their resistance to change; they stay the same unless pushed or pulled very hard.

Many books consider man's problems with society. Some present sharp criticism of established patterns without giving any alternatives. Others propose a utopia impossible to reach. Countless studies in the behavioral sciences assure us, once again, that present conditions, however unfortunate, are extremely difficult to change. Some authors take a more specific tack, although equally fruitless; they tell us with great verbal precision how to solve this or that social problem. The difficulty is that each social problem is not only complex in itself but inter-related with other problems. More, each problem persists because it performs functions for other institutions of society. Most difficult of all, when the problem involves a gain for one group while victimizing another, the suggested solution alerts the gainers and they move to outflank the solution. Building the good society, everyone will agree, presents obstacles of heroic size. And it must be the total society that is transformed; piecemeal tinkering is not enough.

So should we surrender and accept our luckless fate? Should we remain content with our "rich and meaningless world?" Some problems, after all, have been ameliorated during the past century. Some social institutions have bowed to change. So it is that amid the gloomy threat of war, nuclear holocaust, and ecological disaster, some scholars continue to grapple with guided change. One of these is Professor Amitai Etzioni. In 1968 he published a book called *The Active Society* (New York: Free Press) which sets forth the conditions under which man can seek a better society. He asked me to reduce the more than 400,000 words of that volume to some 70,000 words, to make it accessible and intelligible to the undergraduates and the interested and still-hopeful layman. This book is the shorter version.

The Active Society is a book about *guided social change.* It is a difficult book, more empirically grounded than ideological. Embracing an immense volume of behavior in many lands and over long periods of time, it sketches social change under a variety of conditions and emerges not only with an ideal kind of future society (although scarcely a utopia), *but also with an analysis of the path toward it.* The combination of erudition, analysis, and orientation toward an authentic society give the book its significance.

In this shorter version, after three introductory chapters, the reader will find two main sections. The first—Chapters 4–10—deals with the administration of groups and societies as practiced by elites. The focal idea is *knowledge,* that increasingly vital element of modern society. Treatment of criticism of elites opens the way to the second section, which turns to non-elites—mainly *groups challenging the elites and outworn institutions via political action.* Here the focal ideas are public consciousness in the minds of individuals (introduced in Chapter 8), commitment to cherished goals and values, and mobilization.

Mobilization—the quintessence of competition—involves converting assets towards the gaining of power for groups. When these groups, especially "have-not" units, express the aspirations of their members, they gain greater justice, equality, and the other classic goals of man. *Successful mobilization* in a society whose elites are moved to permit flexibility, Etzioni believes, *can lead to the active society*. This is a society in which leaders not only are responsive to their members, but work toward building an authentic structure that facilitates the individual in realizing his full potential.

To produce a book more readable by a wider audience, I have, of course, had to eliminate large chunks of Etzioni's material. Many of the cuts were made in sections dealing with methodology and history and, unfortunately, with international relations. I have used italics and quotation marks copiously for emphasis and a necessarily tight writing style. I did not take the space to indicate all the qualifications and exceptions rightfully due the often complex material, nor did I include a full range of references. The scholar, clearly, will want to stay with Etzioni's book.

The ideas in this one are basically Etzioni's, but I have not refrained from introducing mine when germane. The responsibility, of course, is totally mine. I hope this book is faithful to the original, and will prove to be significant and enlightening to readers who would face an uphill battle in tackling the parent volume. Some of them will graduate to *The Active Society*.

I would like to acknowledge the doughty editorial aid of my wife, Phyllis, and of Mrs. William R. Eddins.

Warren Breed
SCIENTIFIC ANALYSIS CORPORATION
SAN FRANCISCO

CONTENTS

PART THREE

CONTENTS

PART FOUR

PART FIVE

PART I

FOUNDATIONS FOR A THEORY OF THE ACTIVE SOCIETY

CHAPTER I

Potentials for Guided Change in Post-Modern Society*

The *modern* period of history ended with the radical changes in communication, knowledge, and energy that followed World War II. These trends have posed great challenges to the primacy of the *human values* these means are supposed to serve. The *post-modern period*, which (we feel) started in 1945, will witness either further decay of these values or their greater realization to enhance the quality of life. *The active society, one that is master of itself, is a new option available to man in the post-modern period.* An exploration of the conditions under which this option might be exercised is the subject of this book.

A New Direction for Man and Society

Man is reaching a new phase. His capacity to win freedom is greatly extended. But so is his capacity to subjugate other men. Both of these changes follow from his increasing capacity to transform life, rather than accommodate to, *or merely protest*, the social structures he encounters. Earlier barriers that blocked man's quest for self-mastery and social mastery have been tumbling down. *The new discoveries in communication, knowledge, and energy present him with options and new freedom to choose his destiny;* but they also confront him with the choice to destroy everything, even freedom itself.

In the realm of machines, we have witnessed two so-called revolutions: mechanization of work and mechanization of con-

Notes for this Chapter are on page 11.

trol of the machines that work, or cybernation. *In the social realm,* a similar, two-step development has occurred. The first revolution came with the development of the corporation, or modern organization in general, providing a more effective way of "getting things done." The second societal revolution involves cybernetic control by second-order organizations of first-order organizations that do the work—in other words, the introduction of a potential for *societal guidance.*

This "organizational revolution" has a menacing sound. Correctly administered, however, the danger is more sound than fury. In fact, controlling guidance, which prevents drift and inaction by establishing a policy and working to implement it, can be informed by consensus-formation, which works to insure the responsiveness of the controlling elites to the members of society. Thus the active society moves toward its goals: it is active, but not tyrannical.

The advent of the post-modern period has been marked by the rapid rise of a *new technology of knowledge,* which serves data collection and analysis, simulation, and systems analysis. It has been said that the computer is to the production of knowledge what the steam engine was to production of materials. As for *social science,* its exponential growth is illustrated by the statement that "90 to 95 per cent of all the behavioral scientists who ever lived are now alive." [1] In the first two decades of the post-modern period, investment in research and development (R&D) has grown much more rapidly than Gross National Product (GNP), especially in modernized countries.[2] The rapid rise of organizations specializing in the production and processing of *knowledge* is a post-modern parallel to *economic development,* which typified the earlier period of "modernization." As a result, society knows much more about itself, hence the rise in options for social control, new decisions to be made, and a new range of processes to be guided.

That men and groups are increasingly seizing these new options is clear. The rise of "the knowledge industry" (see Chapter 7) and mass education is coupled with the worldwide and instant documentation of new ideas and actions via the mass media, bringing doubled and quadrupled awareness of man by man.[3] Thus protests and demands by Negroes may set off protests by students in a dozen cities and more indirectly inspire demands from welfare recipients for greater benefits, thus eventually calling attention to the campaign for a guaranteed annual income. The new options result not merely in new Presidents and administrations, but in *wholly new institutions, more responsive to more segments of the population.* As new groups rise, grow bigger, and play a greater part in the whole society, so do values change. Thus college seniors move toward the service professions, rather than toward business positions which would pay them much more money;[4] leading business groups adopt a stronger sense of "social responsibility."[5] There seems no end to these weighty changes coming on at an exponential rate. For example, children's IQs are found subject to dramatic climbs if the children are tutored from the time they learn to walk; the potential for both intelligent action and guidance is incalculable.[6]

Also growing is an awareness of the ability to restructure society. Western nations have gained confidence, with their ability to prevent wild inflations and deep depressions and to spur economic growth. Attempts at more "social" reforms, of course, have not as yet been successful—to alter the distribution of wealth, to modify relations between status groups like Negroes and whites, to foster mental health and birth control, to design bonds between nations—but the very attempts in these areas show new daring in social engineering. The more mature communist nations, having learned from earlier failures—"Great Leaps"—are conducting their transformation efforts more realistically and with less cost.

Whether this potential increase in self-guiding controls will be realized, no one can say. Nor do we know whether these efforts will result in more authentic participation by more persons or in greater domination by a powerful few. It is clear, however, that the transition to the post-modern society has begun and will continue.

We shall examine this new potential in the chapters that follow. We shall see that there are imbalances blocking the way. The gap between information and the analysis of that information, for instance, is large and expanding. And well-informed decision-makers are often quite unable to mobilize the members of society; other leaders are unresponsive to members' needs. The new knowledge and the capacity for control may be coupled either with inadequate political skill or with a political will that is too narrowly based.

In sum, this study sets forth ways in which the active society differs from passive and modern societies, provides indicators of a transition in a self-guiding direction, and suggests conditions under which this transition may be initiated, advanced, or blocked.

Societies Changing Themselves

What is needed to make an active society? Social scientists have generally seen "the social code" as set and locked: Societies move through stages, as from folk to urban. Urbanization and modernization are recent examples; they are viewed as processes that cannot be halted.

Our active-passive dimension cuts across these traditional social-science categories. *A basic new distinction is created for social science:* Social units standing above the ongoing processes and seeking to bring them under scrutiny and control. To be active is to be in charge; to be passive is to remain under the control of ongoing forces. The fact is: *Social laws can be altered.* It is here that we find the key to a secular conception of man. This is the ability of men to change themselves by changing their social combinations. By doing this they become the creator. And, the re-creator.

The active social unit may be a community, an association, or a society. It is *always social:* The way to mastery over the world is by joining with others. The romanticists' idea of the fearless hero who masters his fate in a peerless solo act fails to grasp reality. *Social change is chiefly propelled by groups.* The group is not a random collection of stray individuals. It is organized; some lead and others follow, but each plays a role and together they can become active and meet their goals.

The group or society need not be oppressive, as many experts (including Freud) have claimed. The group can be run to meet the needs of its members, for it is part of the individual person as he himself defines his identity. Many groups, of course, are oppressive; we ask, must this continue? History, as we will point out more than once, chronicles many challenges to ruling groups and practices, and shows that seemingly invincible elites often have been overcome. A basic question for us is the *means of change* and its consequences for the members of society.

The active society would be more malleable (more changeable, with greater plasticity) than existing societies. It becomes more responsive to its members, more receptive to its own values.

All societies to date have fallen short of achieving their values. If the new options are to bring this active society closer to a realization of its values, new energy must be injected into societal activities. Harnessing societal energy is the societal equivalent of the physicists' harnessing of nuclear energy. Unleashed in an explosion, it becomes the most destructive force ever known. *Released gradually and employed in men's service, it can change human life.* We believe that locked in social groups is enough energy to achieve a broad realization of values. What should be studied, then, are ways of mobilizing and channeling this latent energy.

The active orientation has three components: (1) a self-conscious and knowing actor (the social unit or group); (2) one or more goals he is committed to realize; and (3) access to levers (or power) that allow resetting of the social code.

Without consciousness the collective actor is unaware of his identity, his being acted upon by others, and his ability to act—his power. He is passive, a sleeping giant. Without commitment to a purpose, action lacks direction and merely drifts.

Without power, awareness and commitment produce no action. *To be active is to be aware, committed, and potent.*

With these three capacities, the active society may guide its path toward the realization of its goals. The active orientation, however, also requires self-restraint. To know is to delay action until information is collected and analyzed. To be committed is to defer rewards in favor of realization of goals. To apply power for activation, as we shall see, is to use it within limits determined by, and in the service of, shared values—not individually held ones. Clearly, a "head" or control center will be needed to apply these capacities to the task. Control is needed for balance; for example, if power tears itself loose from the first two components, consciousness and commitment to goals, action becomes a blind, brute force, and the self-guiding society languishes.

What social forms must the active society possess, what social structures? We have emphasized that joint activity will be required, rather than individual solo performance. Values not mediated through concrete groups become tenuous and frail, (as in "mass society"). Groupings must be built, although not community for community's sake—that would be a retreat from engagement, consciousness, and effective action. The effort to activate and to seek for value realization is also a search for and an exploration of an active social structure. We will examine these groups in Chapter 3.

The Dangers of Activation

If the active society can raise the quality of social life, so also is the road toward it pitted with dangers. When activation is elevated to an ideological level, it may become an unethical and anti-intellectual force. The world knows a number of fascist traditions which preached, "Act now, think later." Mussolini said, "Fascism desires an active man, one engaged in activity with all his energies." [7] Our version of the active orientation is entirely different: Knowledge, commitment, consciousness, and power, coupled with mechanisms for genuine consensus-formation, lead directly away from fascism, not toward it.

The increase in social options could also lead to a further dehumanization of man. The chemical control of behavior may be harnessed for demeaning as well as liberating purposes. The history of recent centuries has shown the paradox of growing technological efficiency and greater productive capacities, but these potential gains have often been linked with social blights: the domination and manipulation of the many by the few, demagoguery for the perpetuation of unresponsive oligarchies and the vulgarity of much of the mass media, obsession with material objects and gimmickry, crowding in big-city ghettoes, and in general the widespread alienation of multitudes. An important part of our sketch of the active society, therefore, will deal with possible means of scotching this paradox and building checks into our model.

A Dynamic Social Contract

The active society writes a dynamic social contract, not a Lockean one, fixed for all time. It is open to amendment, revision, and reformulation, as new forces and options appear. The *changing forces* are the previously passive and underprivileged groups (whether they be peasants, unskilled workers, office workers, students, housewives, or members of minority groups), the spread of consciousness, the expansion of options, the greater vision in more persons, and—most gradually—a decline in the emphasis on material wealth in favor of increased symbolization in society.

In the process of societal activation, not only do more persons participate in society, thereby reconstituting its structure, but the members themselves are transformed. More options, more individuality—and in turn, increasing involvement in more roles, public as well as private. People become more interesting, to themselves and to others. Far less are they carbon copies. The general will of the active society is not merely a reflection of its members at a point in time; the active members change the society, advance the general will, and rely on the change to advance themselves. None of this proceeds at breakneck speed. Human beings cannot reweave anew the normative fabric of society each morning; institutionalization is necessary and inevitable. A delicate balance is required between a general will that is too weak to serve as a solid base for societal growth and one that is too powerful and unresponsive to the members' attempts to bring change.

The dynamic social contract brings an order that is orderly but moving, open to change. The active society contains a changing normative and political consensus, one whose growing value-realization hinges on a continual interplay between members and structure.

The Clarifying Role of Social Science

Knowledge affects each of the components of the active orientation. *Social science* feeds society factual information and analytical perspective, adding to the consciousness of society. Social sciences play a growing part in social activation. As a critical evaluator of social life, as an explorer of alternative structures and their transformation, as an intellectual process freighted with normative commitments—as all of these, social science is able to clarify basic commitments and to make them more realistic and thus more sustained. Social science need not see the world as static and determined; rather, society should be seen as flux, an order to be understood and moved toward the goals of man.

As we shall argue, to know is to have power—and social knowledge is an ever-increasing source of power over society. The more malleable society becomes and the more valid and comprehensive the social sciences become, the greater will be their potential power. It is for this reason that an active orientation among social scientists assumes increasing importance. For social scientists face the temptation of using their knowledge in the narrow interests of the few against the many. There are many safeguards against this danger (chiefly, the sharing of a professional ethic), but an active orientation gives further muscle to professionalization.

The question is, How competent and responsible to society as a whole will social science be? Its knowledge is increasingly being put to use; its quality and its "service for whom?" are the questionable elements.

Our study, overall, is the exploration of a society that knows itself, is committed to moving toward a fuller realization of its values, commands the levers such transformation requires, and is able to set limits on these changes. That would be the active, self-guiding society.

In order to visualize this active society, however, we first need a theory, one that incorporates the basic concepts of the social sciences while allowing for the greater dynamism and potential transformations of the active society.

NOTES

*Detailed references will be found in *The Active Society*, pp. 16–18.

1. Robert K. Merton, "The Mosaic of the Behavioral Sciences," in Bernard Berelson (ed.), *The Behavioral Sciences Today* (New York: Harper & Row, 1964), p. 249.

2. United States Bureau of the Census, *The Statistical Abstract of the United States* (Washington, D.C.: Government Printing Office), for 1959, p. 495; and for 1966, pp. 320, 322, and 543.

3. Marshall McLuhan, *Understanding Media* (New York: McGraw-Hill, 1964).

4. *Newsweek*, May 2, 1966, p. 85—reporting a poll by Louis Harris.

5. Francis X. Sutton *et al.*, *The American Business Creed* (Cambridge: Harvard University Press, 1956).

6. John Leo, "I.Q.'s of Underprivileged Infants Raised Dramatically by Tutors," *New York Times*, Dec. 26, 1968; Jerome S. Bruner *et al.*, *Studies in Cognitive Growth* (New York: Wiley, 1967); and issues of *Child Development*.

7. Mussolini, *The Doctrine of Fascism*, quoted in Carl Cohen, *Communism, Fascism and Democracy* (New York: Random House, 1962), p. 350.

CHAPTER II

Theories of Society—Old and New*

What are the goals of the active society? Our answer is: Goals are to be established by the members of the active society themselves. We know of no guaranteed "seal of approval" which blesses any one set of goals.

Yet from Solon to modern times men have grappled with the question of ideal man in ideal society. Today, most scholars tend to accept some version of those values memorialized by the Enlightenment philosophers of the 18th century. These revolve around freedom, justice, equality, and the dignity of the individual. Whether these values will remain as beacons to guide the active society, however, is not clear. The new knowledge-capacity we have mentioned (and will examine more closely in Chapters 4–7) may change these ideals. The important thing is that man's goals should be determined, and changed, by man.

Constraints—Even Upon Power

Man can never be totally free. He needs some form of social order to maximize his freedom. The young person generally internalizes the patterns of his culture and the more specific roles he is expected to play. These patterns, in turn, have been institutionalized in the society; most members accept them most of the time—although they are constantly undergoing transition.

Thus the individual and the group are *constrained* by many things—tradition, laws, threatened actions by co-workers

Notes for this Chapter are on page 19.

or by competing groups, conscience, expectations by others about how one is supposed to behave—all kinds of obligations.

This recital would represent a "conservative" position were it not for one crucial aspect of guidance theory. Specifically, we hold that *even the elites in power are subject to constraints and social controls.* No "divine right" protects a president, a military-industrial complex, or even a dictator, from many constraints inherent in the fact of organized society. Slaves, peasants, workers, and women have revolted against what they feel is non-moral power; even the brilliant device of the Indian brahmins—granting themselves top position via powerful religious underpinnings—has recently been challenged. One constraint on elite power we will emphasize is consensus-formation, which moves upward from the grass roots to advise the elites on the preferences of the people about the goals they prefer.

Our discussions of knowledge, consciousness, power, mobilization, and consensus-formation, which constitute the thrust of our argument, will attempt to document this point throughout the book. We will suggest that post-modern society holds *options for change—more options than are usually recognized.*

Theories of Society

The theory of the active society builds, of course, upon existing theories. We will describe and criticize the three main types of theories which have attempted to analyze the properties and dynamics of society and then outline the foundations of the social guidance approach. What we are looking for is a theory that will recognize the nature of society while giving it a dynamic that will permit its transformation toward the greater capacity to reach its goals.

THE ATOMISTIC APPROACH

The atomistic approach explains social life in terms of the

properties, relations, and actions among social groups, with no consideration of overall power. For example, the full-competition model of economics, from Adam Smith to this day, explains the national economy by reference to individual persons, families, or firms. If the government appears at all in the analysis, it is seen as being *merely another unit* in the unguided market. In international relations, the balance-of-power theory uses atomistic language.[1] War is the result of a new coalition among various nations or of changes in their relative power. No international organization is given important consideration in the approach. Our approach borrows little from this theory.

THE COLLECTIVISTIC APPROACH

In the collectivistic approach, widely favored among sociologists, especially the functionalists, the units under study are tied to each other with powerful bonds, so that the resulting entity has a "structure," "pattern," or "character." This social unit is capable of reacting creatively to external stimuli. Collectivistic theory does not systematically recognize, however, a capacity of the system to change itself or to restructure social relations on any level.[2] Rather, *social processes unfold without any active control,* as when ethnic relations are said (by Robert E. Park) to move through a "natural history" from conflict through competition and cooperation to assimilation. No unit or supra-unit is assumed to be able to stop—*or accelerate*—the ongoing process. Social systems are viewed as biological ones in which a rise in temperature, say, triggers a higher rate of counteracting perspiration, without any possibility of a deliberate decision to choose any other response. The "social thermostat" maintains a moving equilibrium. Such a quasi-organic model may be suitable for studying primitive or "folk" societies, but empirical observation indicates that *most societies do change themselves* to some degree. Therefore, our theory should include a statement of the nature of the mechanisms that bring about this change.

THE VOLUNTARISTIC APPROACH

This approach sees a societal actor who, in principle, is able to remold his world at will. Some constraints on his freedom are recognized, but these are viewed as abnormalities, restrictions on his true capacity, or remnants of earlier periods. Most voluntaristic theories are a-structural. Their actor is a "great man," or a group of men who act like one man (the "power elite"), or man writ large—"American sensibilities were offended"—as though societies or corporations were giant individuals.[3] Thus society is made to appear monolithic, and *key questions are avoided:* What mechanisms provide for action in unison, what binds the social units, and what allows for the restructuring of their relations and dynamics. Discerning few external or internal constraints on action, the voluntarists' view is hyperactive.

Voluntarism can be found in numerous schools of thought. There was the international relations approach which believed that changes in international law, charters, and international organizations could fundamentally alter world reality. Add cybernetics and game theory, and the "formal organization" approach to the study of public administration.[4] Other forms of voluntarism include psychoanalytical interpretations of national character, communications theories, and studies of military strategy and foreign policy.[5]

If the atomistic approach is likened to Adam Smith's village marketplace, the collectivistic approach is well suited to describe a simple folk society, and voluntarism captures the essence of the army. None of these theories gives post-modern man the purchase to go about transforming his society toward the realization of his—and its—goals.

THE THEORY OF SOCIAL GUIDANCE

We will now sketch a fourth approach—the theory of social guidance. It grows out of the convergence of collectivistic and voluntaristic traditions, but adds several elements. *The result makes the collectivistic approach more active and the voluntaristic one less hyperactive.*

We ask: Which actors, using what means and pursuing what goals, *can change the structure of their system and its boundaries, and what constraints are faced?* We see constraints on actions as fact, resulting from the plurality of social units and contending ideas making up a field of action.

While, obviously, not all groups are "active," we suggest that a theory of social process must include concepts that allow for such a capacity. This is far from the collectivistic assumption that units are related in such a way that no one unit can move significantly without the movement of the others. To correct this passive view, we draw on the cybernetic voluntaristic approach for a conception of controlling units which can exert power to guide the member-units, responding to them and affecting them.

We will feature several concepts that have been avoided in sociology: information, consciousness, decision-making, policy, and strategy. Such concepts as these form the "theory gap" we have been criticizing and prescribing a remedy for.

Some Terms

In this chapter several terms are being used which may require brief comment. For other terms, consult the index.

Actor can be a person or a group as large as a society, if it is the "social unit" under discussion.

Controlling overlayer is a term taken from cybernetics, and here refers to the men and groups of men who receive and evaluate incoming information, make decisions, and issue directions to "social units" in the "controlled underlayer" who carry out the tasks of the acting group. The overlayer is typically composed of *elites* and their staffs.

Supra-unit refers to an actor at the "head" of a social hierarchy, such as a *"controlling overlayer."*

Cybernetics was originally used to refer to the "steering" of groups of machines in mechanical and electrical systems. It is now used to describe communications, both "down" from the elites and "back up" from working units to elites. The upward signals can be part of consensus-formation and provide information so that elites may be more responsive to member units.

Societal is used as the "society-wide" form of "social."

Structure refers to any arrangement or patterning of parts which form an interrelated *system.*

Unit is used here as the most general term for the social molecule. It can refer to a husband-wife pair or a society, and it is frequently used to mean a group, association, bureau, or the like.

Options as a Lever of Change

We have criticized collectivistic (functionalist) approaches on the matter of *social constraints,* in that these limitations are viewed as given, fixed, ongoing processes not subject to change by men's action. And we found voluntarism guilty of paying little attention to these constraints, either internal or external. Guidance theory recognizes constraints as facts of social life, whether they be ideologies, the actions of other groups affecting the one under study, or structural factors within the group, such as control by an established oligarchy. These influence the policy choices made by an elite.

To understand these policy choices requires examination of the paths groups have followed in the past, as well as the alternatives they considered *but rejected,* for whatever reason. The inclusion of these unchosen alternatives has two advantages. It shows the range of man's freedom to guide his affairs, to overcome tradition, and it tells us about the nature of the guidance mechanisms—the question of "how" groups prosper, survive, or die. In short, all forms of "social determinism"—widespread in most theories—have undesirable side-effects, rendering the theory more passive than the facts warrant. The failure to recognize constraints as "drags" on action, as well as a range of choices for future decisions, makes analysis static and passive.

A Contribution to Functional Analysis

Earlier functional theory (e.g., that of Malinowski and Radcliffe-Brown) made several assumptions that gave functional analysis a static and conservative flavor. But there is no need to assume that every item of behavior performs a function or that dysfunctional consequences are to be avoided at all costs.[6] Neither must we swing to the other extreme, to the theory that assumes conflict and coercion.[7] We use both, as in physics, in which both the corpuscle and the wave theories of light are used simultaneously. Note, however, that in both fields the dual approach is a measure of despair for lack of theory which might unite all processes. Our aim in these pages is to suggest that *such despair may be premature.*

Most functional analysis is still collectivistic, emphasizing the interdependence of the parts in a system and ignoring the alternatives, counter-norms and strains always present in social systems. But it has no systematic answer to what we are emphasizing: the question of the rise of new structures and how they come about.

What we are doing here is adding the concept of "options" to functional analysis.[8] *A post-modern society has the option to change its course.* No society must be shackled to an age-old form as is true, for the most part, in biology. In this light, two more propositions occur. Some alternatives are more readily available than others; and, as a rule, no two options have either the same costs or the same consequences. These, in turn, have been affected by earlier choices, and by opportunities which were neglected, or rejected, by the acting group. Again we are linking a structural-functional approach with a genetic (or time-oriented) one, and a more historical with a more analytical one. Here we have the underpinning for our opening hypothesis: that the active society is an option of the historical transition from the modern to the post-modern era.

The course of action any group takes is not viewed as leading mechanically from one "stage" to another, as many theories hold (e.g., Marx, Comte, Spencer). On the contrary, a group or society possesses other options. Whether or not it *exercises* them will have an effect upon history. Thus history can be studied by examining a system composed of several groups or societies, and examining structures, processes, and relations between the units and the choices made (and not made) by them—and how these affect subsequent acts.

Having argued that society can be self-guiding as its elites probe the creation and exploitation of new options, we now turn to the study of groups and the foundation of social order.

NOTES

*Detailed references will be found in *The Active Society*, pp. 16–18.

1. Paul Seabury (ed.), *Balance of Power* (San Francisco: Chandler, 1965).
2. See, e.g., Talcott Parsons and Neil J. Smelser, *Economy and Society* (New York: Free Press, 1956).
3. See James M. Buchanan, "The Pure Theory of Government Finance," *Journal of Political Economy*, Vol. 57 (1949), pp. 496–505.
4. For a review, see Lucian W. Pye, "Personal Identity and Political Ideology," *Behavioral Science*, Vol. 6 (1961), pp. 205–221.
5. Martin Shubik (ed.), *Game Theory and Related Approaches to Social Behavior* (New York: Wiley, 1964).
6. Robert K. Merton, *Social Theory and Social Structure* (New York: Free Press, 1957), Chap. 1.
7. Ralf Dahrendorf, "Out of Utopia," *American Journal of Sociology*, vol. 64 (1958), pp. 115–127.
8. For a thorough treatment of this issue see Walter Buckley, *Sociology and Modern Systems Theory* (Englewood Cliffs: Prentice-Hall, 1967).

CHAPTER III

Elements of Guidance Theory

In this chapter we will attempt to answer two key questions: Who are the carriers and regulators of societal action, and what are the relations among them? These queries take us beyond the three "existing" theories sketched in the preceding chapter. *Collectivistic* theories expect social organizations to reflect the social and cultural background. *Voluntarists* expect groups to be relatively free to act, disregarding their anchorages to their societal base. *Our belief* is that active, self-guiding groups and societies can forge a power of their own, a power which places society on the road to its goals. The dynamism of the active society can transform "culture," "norms," and "structure" so that *barriers may be removed from the solution of social problems which linger on, virtually immune, in the passive society.*

We will first describe three ways in which social relationships are regulated, in terms of the authority over the system—a very important set of distinctions. Then we will discuss social groups: their internal structure, their relations to groups external to them, and their potentialities for change and greater activeness.

Three Bases of Social Order

There are three basic ways for humans to establish order in social groupings—ways in which social atoms may be built into social molecules. A relationship may be *normative, utilitarian,* or *coercive.* A *normative* relationship is cemented by shared norms and values. The members treat each other as goals; the interests of the other person are held to be important by the actor. Mutual commitments are nonrational. High levels of normative order are found within families, religious orders, and stable communities. In *utilitarian* relations, the actors treat each other as means, and commitments are rational. Relationships "pay off," each party gaining from an exchange; the market is a prime example. *Coercion* involves the use, or the threatened use, of means of violence. Actors treat each other as objects, and the commitment may be either rational or nonrational.

In any concrete case, there is a mixture of the three forms. One tends to dominate, however, as in the mother-child relationship, a business relationship, or war. The three basic types of bonds make for differing kinds of social interaction. Cooperation is most likely in the first, competition or contained conflict in the second, and uncontained conflict in the third. Each of the three forms, it is important to note, serves as a base for both integration and cleavage. The very act of binding simultaneously creates a boundary. Shared values and sentiments foster cooperation and cohesion within a group, but each "membership" creates a non-membership, an out-group. Thus the unification of the German states also generated new cleavages in Europe and deepened old ones. And the formation of a shared-interest group may lead to the rise of a counter-interest group. We will use these three forms of order often in this book.

Our task now is to see how men organize themselves into groups which are at once cohesive and controlled. *Cohesion* within a group, large or small, confers the capacity to build consensus and thus movement toward new policies. *Control* provides the capacity to guide the unit, implying a strong calculative element. To start, we will briefly discuss the notion of "groups" and then introduce an important, but little-discussed, type of macroscopic group called the collectivity.

Social scientists usually deal with groups on a range from small to large. There are primary or informal groups, composed of a handful of persons sharing intimate, face-to-face relationships and normative bonds. Then there are larger "formal organizations"—business corporations, battalions, trade unions, civic clubs, recreational groups, churches, action groups, and so on. The largest social group is the society. We believe that there is one more, an intermediate form, of great significance in political action—the collectivity.

The Collectivity

The *collectivity* is larger than an organization but smaller than a society. It has great potential to act, more than a "class" as seen by the Marxists. This potential is based upon a set of *normative interests shared by its members.* It is composed of a number of like-minded social categories, such as urban working-class and ethnic groups on the one hand or business interests sharing a utilitarian, suburban, Protestant orientation on the other. Its stratification position is often horizontal, but may be vertical (as in a civil war) or diagonal (as with many ethnic groupings in the U.S.), crossing lines of social class.

Normative bonds are required to unify the collectivity; utilitarian ties are insufficiently stabilizing for this purpose. Most collectivities are ecologically dispersed (e.g., U.S. Jewry, American Negroes). The members of one almost never interact face-to-face with members of another. They are often multifaceted; that is, members who share one status (e.g. ethnic) will tend also to share others (e.g. religious), though there will always be numerous dimensions on which the members differ.

Having similar interests or values provides only a potential for action. *Mobilization of this potential* is *typically accomplished by an organization,* such as a labor union or a political party. A collectivity without such organizational arms remains passive. Youth groups sharing a common philosophy at the end of the 1960s had moved toward the status of a collectivity, but were having trouble forming an effective organizational arm.

How do collectivities acquire the normative bonds which cement the members together? First, they are composed of smaller groupings which are themselves cohesive. But in order that the potential be turned into coalitions and societal muscle, the loyalties developed in smaller groups must be extended to the larger ones. This depends upon (1) the leaders of the several sub-units, small and large; (2) shared values and symbols; and (3) institutionalized communication channels.

There is no one "great" leader of a collectivity, usually no president or chairman. Often there are several leaders of varying status, and these men interact with each other and with the various related groups. Thus, for instance, American Jewry contains a variety of religious organizations but no one supreme center; yet the extent of coordination and of shared basic values seems sufficient for it to qualify as one collectivity. The same is true for the American "radical right," although the candidacy of George Wallace in 1968 gave it a temporary center. A leadership network is the prime mechanism for extending loyalties, we suggest; symbols and values frequently are epitomized by individual leaders. They often interact together, sometimes are trained at the same institutions (e.g., Oxford and Cambridge). Loci for the interaction can be recreational, as in sailing out of Cowes and Newport decades ago. There is also wide interaction among lieutenants and members, as at conventions, and through the formal communications media (e.g., the Negro press).

Opposing collectivities almost never meet head-on, the way football teams meet on the field. Indeed, a central hypothesis of this study is that direct interaction among the members of two or more collectivities is relatively infrequent, and of little importance when it does occur. For example, Negroes and whites interact more within than between groups, and the same is true for management and labor; they often "talk past each other."

AN EXAMPLE: THE NEGRO GROUPING

An example of a collectivity and its organizational development is the Negro movement in the U.S. For more than 200 years this was a "category" of many individuals taking little action in unison. American Negroes shared many attributes: their race and color, first and foremost, and also a history of slavery and discrimination, a rural farming background, lower class, southern, and Protestant. Some differed, of course, on some of these facets; some were "free men of color," or urban, Catholic, middle-class (the Black Bourgeoisie), and so on. The similarities facilitated normative bonds among them. But although sub-groups existed (fraternal, recreational and especially their churches), interaction was low and thus control networks were weak. Some communication knit them, like the Negro press, but travel was mostly on a north-south axis of migration. Conferences between leaders of the several sub-units were infrequent. Until the 1960s the NAACP and the Urban League constituted the principal organizational networks. All this passivity changed, and rapidly, however, with the Montgomery bus boycott led by Martin Luther King, followed by the sit-ins of 1960 and the "explosion" of the civil rights movement. At this point Negroes seized the initiative from liberal whites and built diverse organizational arms (SNCC, CORE, and the like), and an active collectivity was formed. As in other collectivities, rifts began to appear in the middle 1960s, as Negroes gained assets and power and questions arose about goals, relationships with other groups, means of action, and the rate of acceleration of the movement. Consensus-formation had not caught up with the momentum of the activity.

To gain action potency, these large groupings must organize themselves. A class or ethnic grouping does not easily "rise," ready to man the barricades. When the grouping moves to act, there is deliberate organizational strength behind the action. Such organization is spearheaded by a controlling elite, which makes decisions and issues commands to its component action units. Thus central objects of study are (1) the integration of smaller units into collectivities and societies and (2) the linking of units by control networks into organizations and states. We will again see the significance of the collectivity in Chapter 14.

The State as a Guiding Center

Much of what we have said about the relationship between collectivities and organizations may be applied to the relationship between societies and states. A society without a state (and its "governing" functions—as in "the three branches of government") is largely passive. It is a large aggregate of persons and sub-units with a relatively common culture and geographical boundaries. When the "state" controlling network takes command, however, the society possesses a guiding center. The state is more of a mechanism of "downward" political control than a mechanism of "upward" consensus-formation. The state sets a context which constrains members (the various government agencies, business firms, labor unions, and so on) or provides a base for them to build on. *The state, however, is more than "just another" supra-organization.* Its dominion is more universal, creating for most individuals in it at least a minimal role—that of "citizen." Second, whereas most organizations remain somewhat competitive with other organizations, the state claims a form of monopoly in the kinds of powers it exercises, and it can call upon the use of force to implement its decrees.

We have built our discussion around *cohesive relations* and *control networks* as our two main independent variables. From the viewpoint of a theory of societal guidance, any unit may have a given amount of either one, but *an active unit has a greater amount of both elements.* Our dependent variables, then, are the "activeness" of the unit and its capacity to build consensus, as well as its malleability.

Cohesive units without control networks lack the capacity for self-guidance—are passive; folk societies are a good example.

Units without a cohesive base, on the other hand, possess deficient abilities to build consensus. They can serve as coercive or utilitarian organizations (prisons and craft unions, for example), but not as efficient tools of societal and political action; these require a strong normative element. It is important to note that *any social unit may change;* it can become less structured (or stable) and more organized (active), and vice versa.

Two Types of Autonomy

From the narrow "functionalist" viewpoint, who *controls* a group is irrelevant, as long as the group's needs are met. But members of the group often care very much: the search for "independence" plays a big part in history. Two quite different meanings of "independence," however, must be distinguished. *Functional self-sufficiency* means that the group is taking care of all its needs. The same group, however, might be dominated by another group—might not be *autonomous.* The active, self-guiding society has both these qualities, functional self-sufficiency and autonomy. It can set its own goals and is optimally prepared to achieve them.

These two qualities may vary independently of each other. A colonial society, for example, is not autonomous but may be taking care of its own needs quite well. Thus in studying how groups relate to one another, we can focus on these *imbalances.* Certain tensions are brought about by imbalances, often bringing a group to seek to restore the balance, to bring fundamental social change. This is another way of saying that a group's internal relationships are related to its relationships with other groups, and vice versa.

Imbalances in Autonomy

One frequent type of imbalance is the combination of high autonomy in normative activities with less autonomy in utilitarian ones. Most colonial societies showed this pattern, and their national independence movements sought to restore the balance. (Even when they have gained autonomy, of course, we do not expect that they will soon become active.) Studies of prisons reveal that inmates, who are granted little utilitarian autonomy, are able to maintain high normative autonomy; the authorities' attempts to establish rules for interpersonal behavior are largely ignored. Thus an imbalance exists, and the inmates work to attain balance. They attempt to do this by gaining control of utilitarian means (smuggling food from the outside, producing whiskey, and "fixing," so that the guards will perform according to norms set by the inmates). A final example of a unit subject to external control which works to internalize it, thus restoring balance, is seen in adolescence. Here tension grows as normative autonomy is gained by the youth while parents maintain utilitarian controls. The tension is rarely completely resolved until the young person obtains his own home and job, so that his utilitarian autonomy approximates his normative independence.

These two kinds of dependence also clarify a related question: conditions under which people revolt. Common sense suggests that the most oppressed peoples will revolt, but this is not borne out in fact. Social scientists have replaced this notion with the proposition that improved conditions bring on rising expectations, and violent uprisings may occur if additional improvements are stalled. It has also been suggested that imbalances in the available assets, not their absence, is the key variable. Societal guidance theory suggests, on the other hand, that rebel fervor stems more from imbalances in self-control than in assets. In the French Revolution, for example, it was not frustrations over shifts in the standard of living but the refusal by the elites to grant continued participation in the political process that triggered the revolution.

So far we have discussed the shift from external to internalized control and the balancing of self-controls and self-sufficiency. A parallel process is the loss of control by a previously dominating group, and the consequent effect on the group itself. The recent history of decolonization shows that Britain, France, and Belgium have differed in the relative success of their dissociation from the colonial structure. Britain is viewed as the most successful. In France the loss of colonies is associated with both instability and the semi-authoritarian regime of de Gaulle. For Belgium, withdrawal was followed by intensification of the internal conflict between the two rival linguistic-cultural collectivities. We can conclude that some societies are more capable than others in reallocating internal control.

Two Kinds of Change

These processes—imbalances and shifts—assume a capacity for societal change. And change can and does come about in these ways. But our interests in this book pose an important distinction between two kinds of change.

The first kind is *homeostasis.* A social unit is homeostatic if it can generate forces that allow it to maintain its pattern and boundaries in the face of ongoing environmental changes. The second is *transformability.* Possessing this rare quality, a social unit can design a new self-image and thereupon can change its parts and internal relationships as well as its boundaries to create a new, active unit. This it can do *even if the old unit has not yet become unstable.* Not merely content with adapting to the environment and correcting "bit" imbalances, it creates a new pattern, new parts—a new society. This active, self-guiding society then is optimally prepared to seek the realization of its goals and values.

Dangers, of course, beset the transformation process. While "social problems"—malformations, faulty integrations, and unresponsive structures—may decrease, greater difficulties may arise. Transformation frequently requires dissolving the old structure. De-differentiation of groupings along old lines of rewards and statuses must occur, and with it redifferentiation in accord with new values (e.g., equality, justice). Thus during the process, the transformation may be trapped, blocked or derailed, and new elites and scapegoats and patterns of injustice formed. But when transformation is complete, social creativity will be unusually high.

Control Centers and Implementation Mechanisms

Controlling overlayers tend to include two kinds of sub-units: control centers (their "heads") and implementation mechanisms (their "bodies"). *Control centers* (occupied by elites) are units which (1) process incoming knowledge, (2) make major decisions, and (3) issue signals giving orders to acting units. *Implementation mechanisms* link the control centers with the member units under control. Two types of implementation processes generate power to support the signals issued by the control centers and carry messages (to sub-units, feedback from sub-units to elites, input of raw knowledge). The upward (feed-back) signals thus carried should be distinguished from signals carried by *the consensus-formation process.* To illustrate the difference: Corporation HQ is a control center: Up-ward reports by foremen on workers' morale are implementation feedbacks; the representative functions of labor union stewards are part of the consensus-formation process. Note that the "boundaries" of this system may stretch from Wall Street through the Pentagon building to the homes of thousands of employees—an almost infinite mosaic of cross-cutting relation-ships.

Types of Elites in Control Centers

An elite is a control center. Its triple job is to process knowledge, make decisions, and give commands. Persons in the elite need not have "leadership" qualities, so long as they perform the three functions. Further, there is no assumption here of "elitist superiority" of the members; they may be drawn from lower ranks. Relations between elites and sub-units may exhibit many kinds of imbalances and strains.

From the viewpoint of the analysis of controlling overlayers, these distinctions between elites seem productive:

1. *External versus internal elites.* An internal elite is a member of the supra-unit; an external elite is not. Examples of the latter are colonial systems and newly-arrived managers of companies joined in a conglomerate stock merger. With external elites, guidance is less effective and the unit is less active.

2. Elites may be characterized by the kind of activities they control as either *specific* or *general.* If specific, an elite may control, for example, only economic tasks, not religious or educational ones. Unless otherwise specified, our use of the term will imply generalized control.

3. A distinction crucially important for human freedom and the quality of life is that elite control may be *prescriptive* or *contextuating.* Totalitarian control is highly prescriptive, specific about what must and must not be done. Individuals subject to such rule tend to be alienated. Controls in the self-guiding society are contextuating, merely defining the limits within which behavior may vary. We shall have more to say about this.

The Active Society "Processes" Passive Attributes

The previous discussion has made two points: the integration of units into collectivities and societies and the linking of units by control networks into organizations and states.

An active society contains the same raw materials as any other society. *What it adds is the "processing" of these raw materials.* This "transforming" work is illustrated in a table:

Passive attributes, present in all societies	*Forces which "process" the passive attributes to make the active society*
1. Energy, unprocessed, potential	1A. Processing capacity, yielding committed (mobilized) energy.
2. Action underlayer	2A. Controlling overlayer (control centers and implementing mechanisms)
3. Collectivity	3A. Organization ("active" arms)
4. Society	4A. State
5. Cohesive relations	5A. Control networks
6. Societal structure	6A. Organizational pattern
7. Assets	7A. Power
8. Class	8A. Elite

Note that while passive attributes appear on the lefthand side, those on the right are not in themselves "active"; only when they are combined with the passive base is the active quality generated.

In the following chapters we study the specific components of both controlling overlayers and consensus-formation processes and explore the ways in which differences in these forms affect the extent to which a societal unit is active. It is a central belief of the theory of societal guidance that differences in control *and* consensus account for a significant part of the variance in societal activeness and in the transformability of societal units—*not all* of the variance, but a significant part, so that a theory that excludes them is seriously deficient.

Each chapter following deals with one independent variable. Each component of the societal guidance mechanism is studied throughout from these five viewpoints: (1) the controlling *functions* it fulfills; (2) the *processes* it uses; (3) the *structure* of the units which specialize in serving the particular function(s); (4) the *relations* between these units and other units; and (5) changes in all these over time, i.e., *genetically*.

It should be stressed that the following discussion advances propositions about the activeness of units and is not concerned with a review of the literature; illustrations are given when relevant and instructive.

An underlying assumption of all that follows is that without these special processes and units, without the commitment of resources, a unit cannot gain or maintain an active orientation. Without these, passivity abides, and the group's course is determined by ongoing forces. To be passive is natural; it is activeness that requires the effort of men and groups and explanation by social scientists.

PART II

CYBERNETIC FACTORS

CHAPTER 

The Uses of Knowledge*

When a government (or any other large group) commits a blunder, what happened to cause it? Very often the blame is placed upon malevolence, or upon the self-seeking conspiracy of a powerful group, or low IQ's, or the "wrong-headed" ideology of the officials. All of these doubtless play a part. Our position, however, states that very often part of the difficulty is *poor knowledge.*

In this, the first of five chapters on knowledge, several questions are put: What functions does knowledge serve for groups? To what extent are societal actors able to gain a valid view of their environment and of themselves? How can small "bits" of knowledge be synthesized to make a "bigger picture"? Must usable knowledge be the "scientific" kind?

To assert that knowledge is a key component in complex society is to say nothing new. It should not be necessary to proclaim the significance of this vital ingredient in a society that relies on education, science, and the need of individuals to understand not only their own specialty but their small place in the dazzling interdependence of millions and billions of other elements.

Nevertheless it does seem necessary. Social scientists, in their quest to understand this fragmented but delicately organized world, have devoted much more attention to power than to knowledge. The decisions that are made to keep the world running and accelerating are seen in terms of men in positions of power. More attention to knowledge will be required in the post-modern world, with new demands and new questions and

Notes for this Chapter are on page 49.

issues that surface and peak with extraordinary speed—an apt case being the speed that "ecology" issues hit politicians in 1969.

With strong knowledge a group or society can more effectively seek its goals. It is freed from responding blindly, or in a traditional fashion, to new conditions. Knowledge is a major source of a society's capacity to guide itself. Neither power nor compassion is enough. Great differences in the quality and use of knowledge distinguish one group or society from another.

Three Examples of Knowledge Failure

One way to demonstrate the importance of knowledge is to describe some notable failures in which poor knowledge played a part. We present three of these.

1. For a tragic instance of an action taken with weak information, consider the U.S. involvement in Vietnam. Increasing commitments were made during the 1960s despite ignorance and misinformation about many things: the history of the area, and especially the loyalties and solidarity of the several tribal and religious groupings; the relationships between these groups and the interests each were seeking; the political sophistication of typical Vietnamese as well as their elites—and the willingness of some to grow extremely wealthy from U.S. input; the problem of public facilities and services in the Saigon area under enormously stepped-up in-migration; the morality of interfering in the internal affairs of another country; the details of the "domino theory" of a communist take-over of all Southeast Asia; relationships between Hanoi, Peking, Moscow, and North Korea; the difficulties of U.S.-type warfare in the jungle—lessons apparently forgotten since World War II; political consequences within the U.S.—e.g. the growing antiwar backlash in 1966–1968 and the withdrawal of President Johnson from an attempt at re-election. Since the escalation, of course, better knowledge has become available, but it came too late to prevent disaster.

2. During the 1960s the U.S. "fought a war on poverty." Few feel it has been successful, and poor knowledge was one of the sources of failure. Knowledge, specifically, about two groups—the target "poverty" groups and the vested-interest groups in the community. During the decade, for example, numerous questions arose about the poor, and not many answers.[1] Who were they—that is, "how far up" the class ladder do we find the poor? Which of them are amenable to aid? What do they themselves want? Do they accept middle-class aspirations? Do they want to rise on the status ladder, and do they have the motivation to start the climb? What kinds of skills and outlooks would equip them best for lives of dignity? How important is the lack of a father-figure in many lower-class families, and how can this be remedied? Or is it a problem of the poor education of parents, the lackluster schools in the slums, discrimination, or association with older delinquents? What corrodes desire and deepens the poverty cycle? Questions of this kind multiply, and the middle-class stance of the would-be helpers provided a nagging, built-in bias of fact and interpretation. To all of these questions, few answers were ready.

Even a greater number of questions came to be asked about the host community and powerful groups and bureaucracies whose cooperation was needed before change could come. A review of the pluralistic stew and the resistance encountered from politicians, school administrations, welfare councils, labor, chambers of commerce, church and educational groups, and the poor themselves suggests the difficulties of understanding community action, let alone bringing about structural change.[2] Knowledge about how to weld these groups—some of whom were profiting from poverty—into a force for tackling poverty at its roots was too scarce for success.

3. When executives of the Ford Motor Company decided in the mid-1950s to build a new automobile—the Edsel—they were certainly hoping to make money: there was no "plot" within the firm to destroy itself. Much attention was devoted to the knowledge problem.[3] More than four years were spent on engineering, styling, and consumer surveys. Six volumes of data

were accumulated to support the go-ahead decision. As is now well-known, after two years the Edsel was discontinued with an estimated loss of $350,000,000. Blame has been assigned to several sources, but one of them was the insufficient attention given to the recently-rising sales of small foreign cars. The powerful new car was built for a market that had gone elsewhere.

And a Success Story: The CEA

Knowledge problems are chronic in modern society, as the examples have suggested. Successes are frequently found in science, both pure and applied. The 1969 moon landing is a notable example. The success of the Council of Economic Advisers is particularly pertinent to this book, because it proves that social-science knowledge can strengthen government.

The CEA was established by the Employment Act of 1946 to give the President and Congress expert advice on economic policy.[4] Being independent both of partisan groups and existing agencies (Budget Bureau, Treasury Department, and the like) and blessed with access to the President, the Council has been able to recruit high-quality staff from universities and research institutes, while keeping in close touch with the regular agencies of government. Thus fitted out, it has played a key role in several areas: levelling the business cycle; reducing unemployment; urging the tax cut of 1964—an extremely successful venture; overcoming outdated preconceptions; educating Presidents and Congress; and in general using both economic theory and data to gain a long-range picture and recommend preventive and remedial actions by government. This was the first academic discipline to gain status as a separate agency on the President's staff. Its success has encouraged other social scientists to seek the establishment of additional expert councils to supply advice and guidance—"social reports," and the like—to the highest levels of government.

One can find occasional exceptions to the rule that groups need knowledge and blunder without it. Hitler's intelligence service was poor, but this did not cost him heavily at first. In one notable error he ordered a large reduction in armaments production three months after he began the Russian campaign.[5] The 1954 school desegregation decision of the U.S. Supreme Court rested its "sociological" foundations—that separation of Negro children from whites "generates a feeling of inferiority" —upon extremely weak experimental evidence.[6] It is reassuring, of course, to add that subsequent research has strengthened the conclusion and in general that good knowledge aids in the gaining of group goals.

Men produce knowledge and use it as a group property. Like other collective assets, it is stored (in libraries and on computer tapes) and is made available for collective action (as when organizations retain experts). In some senses, groups use knowledge much like persons do; their internal structures may bias their views of the world and their changing places in it, so that they may misunderstand the situation and act in error. Not surprisingly, the quality of a group's knowledge reflects the group and its leadership, the autonomy and financial support given to the knowledge bureau, and the lines of communication between the knowledge elites and the decision-makers.

The Functions of Knowledge

Knowledge is a set of symbols that performs two functions for groups and societies. By providing information, it contains a *relation to reality*, to the social and non-social environment. Secondly, knowledge (in conjunction with religion and ideology) provides "meaning," an important bond that ties actors to one another and helps to answer many deep questions beginning with "why?" Meaning is derived by reasoning about facts and by evaluating them against group standards, a function we refer to as *evaluative interpretation.*

CYBERNETIC FACTORS

All actors (persons and groups) have a capacity for *reality-testing.* Like scientists, they revise their knowledge to some degree on the basis of their experience. Yet most people and groups fall short of scientific reality-testing in two ways: their procedures are comparatively loose, and they are relatively more interested in the interpretive aspect of their knowledge, which tends to be incompatible with giving *primary* consideration to reality-testing. Some actors more willingly face reality than others, but in fact no actor's knowledge escapes considerable evaluative interpretation. We hold that *most actors mix pure information and value-judgments,* facts and common sense, science and folklore, old and new bits of information, in a kind of informational-evaluation stew.

Most of the Christian world, for example, was unwilling to accept—or even study—Darwin's theory of natural selection —hence the century-long "monkey controversy" between the scientists and the religionists. Much more recently, people in the Deep South not only were unwilling to listen to pro-Negro arguments, they actively sought to muzzle the dissidents. When a community newspaper in Mississippi, for example, began to devote increasing attention to the issue and satirized racism, advertising and subscriptions dried up, and the editor was eventually driven out of the community.[7]

This is not as damaging, generally, as it might seem. Even the scientist cannot, after all, remain completely "value-free." For others, facts without normative interpretations are of little utility. The recognition that one technology is more efficient than another is no help if it violates the religious values of the group, the national self-image of a society, or the political commitments of an elite. "Sacred cows" of all kinds are clear and present facts of life; they are an important constraint on action. Most often, societal decision-makers will assess new technologies with an eye to both their efficiency and their normative acceptability.

There is no problem when both functions of knowledge are served by the same "bit," when both the reality of the actor's knowledge and his evaluative interpretation are supported by the item. But even when the two functions collide, a compromise is still possible. New information is not necessarily disregarded, but it may be neglected, diluted, or distorted to maintain prevailing values. Further, even the most learned actor seldom has more than a fraction of the relevant information he could use. The study of knowledge and action, therefore, is concerned with *relative* degrees of ignorance, confusion of fact and half-fact, and dissociation of intellect from the guidance of action.

These considerations, often neglected by the rationalists of the new technology of knowledge, explain why the growing improvement in the societal capacity to collect and analyze information has not solved knowledge-to-action problems. This phenomenon is much like the factory slow-down, in which industrial production is more in accord with norms agreed upon by workers than with their physiological capacities. The degree to which the knowledge produced is valid and the extent to which it is utilized are both only partially determined by technical criteria, and other considerations intrude: the social definitions of how much information is desired, what questions are submitted to research, and which findings are to be accepted, suppressed, or disregarded.

All societal actors interpret information. It is this interpretation which *bridges* knowledge and values. Pathological units are those whose reality-testing is so constricted that they can accommodate to changed conditions only at very high cost. One recalls the 1964 presidential campaign of Senator Goldwater and his staff. Unlike other campaigners, they repeatedly violated many of the rules of effective political conduct, despite continued feedback from public opinion polls, press reports, and the advice of supporters.

Limitations on Societal Reality-Testing

There are four reasons why the reality-testing of Macroscopic actors is limited:

1. Macro-actors have a greater capacity to alter their environments than persons (who, it is true, can alter their *perceptions* of conditions). Macro-actors *can change reality itself* to fit their preconceptions—they can start wars to confirm their perceptions of hostile neighbors.

2. A larger amount of "slack" exists between elites and members, as when elites maintain a bipartisan foreign policy. With little debate on the issue, elites are insulated from correctives in the form of comment or criticism.

3. Since knowledge must be shared by the several elites and by active units if it is to guide policy and action, provision must be made for its wide dissemination. Accomplishing this task is not simple; a committee can share readily, but not so easily a society. The degree to which a societal unit's knowledge is shared among elites and active publics is a key criterion by which to measure *societal* knowledge. Greater sharing generally means greater capacity to act, yet high knowledge sharing is not common.

4. A person's reality-testing is reinforced by other persons with whom he interacts, a principle embodied in the interaction theory of Cooley and G. H. Mead.[8] Macro-actors are more distant from each other. The *person* who commits a faux-pas will somehow be chided, or quietly advised by a "best friend," or shunned for a period until he notes the chill. A *nation,* however, may hold a position for years without similar awareness. Since there is comparatively little supranational interaction, there is relatively little feedback sensitivity.

Among nations and among classes, races, or tribes in the many poorly-integrated societies there are few corrective mechanisms to chide the actor. Friendships do exist among macro-actors; Britain, for instance, has often acted as a trusted reality-testing friend for the United States, and Scandinavian diplomats have served in avuncular roles. But the strength of integrative bonds between countries over time in no way matches that existing between old personal friends.

On the macroscopic level, the nearest thing to the friendly act of "taking aside" a momentarily erring person is crisis. The crisis may come naturally, or it may be provoked by a sensational event. Authorities realize they must check their perspective and face reality at such fabled times as these: the Hungarian revolt of 1956 reveals that the U.S. cannot intervene in Eastern Europe, despite much previous talk; students occupy university buildings; Rachel Carson publishes her critique of the misuses of pesticides and their danger to the ecological balance; CBS in 1968 airs an hour-long documentary on malnutrition in the U.S. A crisis, obviously, has a therapeutic effect only if it forces action previously avoided, including the re-evaluation of knowledge. The unit, of course, may react by regressing, by ritualistically repeating earlier moves with increased rigidity. The greater brittleness leaves the unit even more vulnerable than before.

The Validity of Knowledge and Societal Structure

The particular social organization and personnel of a unit obviously affect the quality of its knowledge and the direction in which it is slanted or biased. Both the specific direction of the slanting and the degree to which knowledge is unrealistic depend considerably upon the values and organizational forms of the unit. It works much like the way a person's unconscious mind and superego influence his use of knowledge. And, like psychotherapists, social scientists who would unveil the underlying societal dynamics invite resistance and rejection, because the exposure of latent factors threatens those who benefit from the false images. The official or bureau whose function is obsolescent or whose performance is sapping goal attainment are cases in point.

Processes of personnel selection sometimes recruit personality types who may have greater or lesser capacity to absorb valid knowledge, who are psychologically freer to experiment, or who are able to communicate new knowledge to peers and non-elites. Personal traits well suited to the gaining of high position, whether elective or appointive, may prove inimical to the effective performance of the position once it is attained; film stars and wealthy widows who contribute generously to campaigns come to mind.

We have contended that persons have better "reality-testing" skills and opportunities than macro-units. Yet it is also true that macro-units command much greater quantities of knowledge. Further, they are in a position to gain new knowledge very rapidly. Usually the question of how a unit learns is given in atomistic-individualistic terms: enroll the members in a training course. This, however, is an assumption at the micro-unit or individual level. *A group can learn by importing experts or by purchasing a library of books or tapes.* Thus large units possess more knowledge than is available to any one member (or even of all members combined). And whereas a person has difficulty unlearning material, a unit can do so with relative ease by changing its experts or reprogramming the computers.

The Function of Synthesis

Both information and evaluation tend to be produced bit by bit. Information is built fact by fact, item by item. Evaluation too is often fragmented, although it is a process of assessing items by relating them to broader contexts. Then, too, items are frequently evaluated in terms of a single dimension. The danger is that items assessed as valuable may be so only if complementary items are also available, as with Ford's neglect of rising sales of small foreign cars in the Edsel disaster, or with the undigested data in FBI dossiers.

For knowledge to be usable, as a rule, it must be organized into more encompassing contexts. *This is accomplished by synthesis.* Synthesis is a matter of degree; no actor relates all his knowledge to the whole, but some relate more and better than others. Oddly, even scholars underplay synthesis; they speak much of analysis—studying bits ever more microscopically (as in graduate courses)—but little of synthesis.

To assess the level of knowledge-synthesis, these three dimensions should be known: (1) the number of bits included —generally the more the bits the tougher the task; (2) the number of bits integrated into how many different dimensions and contexts; and (3) the degree to which the contexts are related to each other to make up a knowledge system. High synthesis comes only when bits are well integrated into contexts and contexts into knowledge systems.

The starting point of societal guidance theory for the study of knowledge synthesis is that *bits are not integrated into contexts without investment and effort.*

When knowledge input and synthesizing capacities are out of balance, difficulties arise. When the synthesizing ability of an actor is low, the greater his knowledge input the greater also will be his disorientation. His view of the world and of himself will be splintered—clear in spots but vague overall. Some experts believe that before the attack on Pearl Harbor, various fragmented bits about Japanese actions came across the desks of American diplomats and intelligence officials, but that these officials lacked the mechanisms to correlate the bits into a meaningful synthesis.[9] When knowledge input is small, informal synthesis may suffice. But when input is voluminous and evaluation is complex, these mechanisms become flooded. This is true not only of persons but of organizations; companies bidding for the 900-passenger C–5A transport plane submitted to the Federal Aviation Agency proposals of 240,000 pages, in 480 volumes.[10] Scholars recognize the problem when the flow of information approaches the stage of glut: e.g., the dilemma of the historian of the 20th century.

Whatever the particulars in a given case, the rub is the same. A common reaction to deficient synthesis is for the controlling unit to bury itself in detail and neglect longitudinal and lateral review. Observers agree, for example, that the Department of State has much more effective planning capacities for dealing with single, isolated acts than for formulating overall policy. NASA spends much more money collecting information than analyzing it—a statement one could make about hundreds of organizations, public and private. Scholars applying for research grants seldom allocate enough time in their budget pages for analysis of the data they propose to gather. Piles of pages of computer printouts are the vaguely guilt-provoking bane of many research offices. President Johnson monitored such details of the Vietnam war as the altitudes of bombers and sizes of bombs; his Waterloo resulted from his bit-orientation. There is reason to believe that this is a general pattern of the Anglo-Saxon collective use of knowledge, having deep historical and philosophical roots.[11]

When cognitive and evaluative syntheses are highly segregated, the decision-maker is unaware of the *moral implications* both of his plans for action and of the information he gains about the outcome of his acts. The dissociation of military thinking from political and normative evaluations is a well-known case in point. Conversely, it should be noted that over-synthesis can occur, as with scholasticism.

Sources of Weak Synthesis

Capable synthesizing is rare. Most groups gather more information than they analyze and synthesize. Many otherwise well-organized units score low in synthesis. Yet an active societal unit requires good synthesis, of a quality that matches other knowledge-capacities.

As with many other kinds of actions, the ability for synthesis in a group is affected by the internal makeup of the controlling elites. Some elites give greater importance to synthesis and provide second-order review units which analyze the work of the first-order review units, and so on. The Department of State, with its poor capacity for synthesis, spent $109 million for R&D in fiscal year 1965, compared to $4,555 million spent by NASA, the space agency.[12]

The deeper causes of "flooding"—high information output coupled with low synthesizing capacities—are not to be found in the strategy followed by the sub-units but in the organizational structure itself. Flooding is likely to occur, we suggest, when higher-ranking units command fewer cybernetic resources than the units under their control. Such a discrepancy between formal authority and capacity to regulate is found, for example, in the White House Office of Science and Technology, which has a much smaller staff and budget than the HQ of the agencies it supposedly oversees.[13]

Social conditions making for high information input and low synthesis and, therefore, for low knowledge include the following: (1) the pressure of time and the shortage of resources and skilled personnel, so that synthesis is sacrificed, rushed, or neglected; and (2) political pressures from elites, both inside and outside the group, which may tend to mute some unflattering conclusions. Both factors are reported to have handcuffed such projects as the report of the Warren Commission on the assassination of President Kennedy, the work of the National Commission on Technology, Automation and Economic Progress,[14] and the McCone Commission Report on the 1965 Watts riots in Los Angeles.[15]

Toward Encompassing Knowledge

All knowledge is simplification, as a map is to a road. It reports some details and neglects many others, and the signs must be understood if it is to be useful.

The following criteria are suggested for comparing the extent to which the societal knowledge of various actors services their needs for reality-testing and evaluative interpretation. Societal knowledge can be fruitfully compared according to the extent to which (1) it is empirically valid (bit by bit), (2) the various contexts are synthesized, (3) reality-testing and evaluation are fused or related, and (4) it is encompassing in its coverage.

We suppose that, in primitive knowledge, reality-testing and evaluation are highly fused; in modern knowledge they are relatively segregated and unrelated; and in active knowledge they are less segregated and much more related. Compare for example, the bit-by-bit educational theory of Piaget, who represents the generation before the post-modern era, with that of educationists of the 1960s (Bruner, Neill, and many others) who advocate contextual learning.[16]

The need for knowledge to be encompassing is often challenged. In fact, a narrow specialized focus is often considered an essential prerequisite for the effective production of knowledge. In contrast, we see knowledge as resting in contexts. A long-standing conflict resides here; empiricist-scientists stress "hard facts" and downgrade other intellectual efforts—they undervalue coverage. The humanists, for their part, associate empiricism with escape from evaluative responsibilities. As long as there are some specialists who concern themselves with synthesis, however, societal needs can be served. Thus poets writing about nature, psychoanalysts writing about society, and literary critics writing about international relations have knowledge functions. Their concepts are more encompassing, closer to the world of action, and more evaluative than those of science. The poet who telescopes the bombing of Hiroshima into a sonnet produces a less analytic and less accurate but a more intimate and expressive view than a pollster working on the same phenomenon. The white journalist who darkened his skin and traveled through the Deep South was able to describe "how the Negro feels" more eloquently than a dozen sample studies.[17] Both kinds of perspectives enhance a society's knowledge for both of the functions of knowledge—reality-testing and "meaning."

In sum, *the active society requires much accurate, encompassing, and synthesized knowledge.* Goal attainment depends on policy decisions, and decisions depend on knowledge. The more malleable the unit, the greater its need for an overall design to guide its efforts toward its environment and toward itself. Coverage of expressive aspects of life as well as rigorous cost analysis helps to fuel and maintain active goal seeking. Well-synthesized knowledge nourishes that blessed capacity: vision.

on official dicta, and a pattern of interpretative inferences applied to the official media.[1] Only a few Russians went so far as to believe the exact opposite of what the government said, but many distrusted and discounted the official media. Large costs typically attend major changes in public opinion.

Bits and Contexts in Changing Knowledge

In guiding societal action via adjusting knowledge, elites face costs from two sources. One is technological: the costs of printing or of maintaining radio and television stations. The other is social and symbolic: the beliefs of individuals, which tend to be more or less consistent within the individual and shared by him with his fellows. We suggest that it is fruitful to view societal knowledge as having a hierarchical structure which provides a *contextuating orientation* for bits (or items) of knowledge. The bits are more concrete, specific, and cognitive than the contexts. A fact is a bit; a theory is a context. Our question deals with *ways of changing contexts.*

Bits can be changed relatively cheaply. This assumes, however, that the new bits fit the existing larger context. For example, most Americans in the late 1940s and the 1950s believed the Soviet Union to be a militarily aggressive and expansionist force (a contextuating orientation). Several bits of knowledge (the subjection of Czechoslovakia in 1948, the crushing of the Hungarian rebellion of 1956) were part of the "evidence." (The rejection of totalitarianism, of course, gave a *normative* foundation.) Other people held the same contextuating orientation but supported it with other bits (Soviet intervention in Poland and East Germany in 1953 and Krushchev's 1959 "We shall bury you" speech). Note that we use the active participial form "contextuating" to suggest that the contextual relations among the bits are, in part, open to guided change.

Generally, societal knowledge will change not atomistically—in bits—but contextually, as the bits of evidence are seen to shift the pattern in a new direction. The following propositions, if verified, would support our view of the contextual organization of knowledge: (1) It is more costly to change a contextuating orientation than to replace a bit that fits an orientation with another that does not; and the latter action, in turn, is more costly than replacing a bit that fits with another which also fits; (2) bits can be removed cheaply so long as the context is not challenged, but such removal has few action consequences because support for action is based on context rather than on bits; and (3) when the contextuating orientation is strained by the continual removal of bits, the cost of removing additional bits is expected to rise. With continued removal, the cost will rise sharply until the old orientation snaps. At that point the field can be reorganized relatively inexpensively.

It is not expensive for an elite to introduce a new contextuating orientation in areas in which none has been established. Into the late 1950s outer space was an unimprinted field. When Sputnik orbited in 1957 few Americans had established notions about space. It was not difficult for Presidents Eisenhower and Kennedy to establish a context for it into which later bits could be fit.[2]

Much the same is true for additional specification of a previously vague field. Thus well into this century people over 65 were seen rather vaguely as "old people." Then welfare groups, social scientists, and others began redefining them in the new context as "senior citizens," in a new stage of "growth." Old age was dramatized as a time for leisure and a continued socially active life.[3] The relatively *low cost* of this respecified context is apparent if we compare it, for instance, to efforts to change the societal image of the Jew. The latter, it is true, has also been changed, although at the cost of Hitlerism and a widespread tolerance campaign.

THE KENNEDY EXPERIMENT: AN ILLUSTRATION

To illustrate the *costs* of attempting to alter an institutionalized context, we take the example of the introduction of the foreign policy of detente in 1963–1964.[4] On June 10, 1963, President Kennedy announced the initiation of a major change in the foreign policy of the U.S., calling it "a strategy for peace." This aimed to change the "Cold War" context to which much of the nation had been committed since the late 1940s.

Kennedy noted that "constructive changes" had come about in the Soviet Union which "might bring within reach solutions which now seem beyond us." The Cold War should not be viewed as immutable, he said. "Our problems are man-made . . . and can be solved by man." U.S. policies should encourage the Soviets to believe that a genuine peace would serve their interests. He asked Americans to re-examine their attitudes toward the U.S.S.R. and the Cold War—that is, to be willing to alter their images of others and of themselves. In short, he was calling into question the Cold War context. The political elite was attempting to *guide* public opinion.

Many moves toward the "thaw" followed in the next three months. Kennedy suggested that the U.S. and the U.S.S.R. explore the stars together. The U.S. sold $65 million worth of wheat to the U.S.S.R., the two nations initiated a partial nuclear test ban treaty, and several other "coexistence" measures were agreed upon or discussed. Much debate took place in the mass media and in Congress, and a new mood was noted in newspapers and opinion polls.

By late October 1963 Kennedy was slowing his detente moves. Fewer new measures were begun; Soviet initiatives were turned down; negotiations over pending projects (air travel, a consular treaty, etc.) were delayed. Kennedy seems to have realized, to put it in our terminology, *how strongly the old context was institutionalized* and how costly it would be to change. The test ban treaty had to be ratified by the Senate and various pressure groups were actively agitating against it. His re-election was at stake. Well aware of President Wilson's blunder, Kennedy did not wish to sign a treaty which the senate might not ratify.

Before he would sign it and until it was ratified, he had much to do. He personally coordinated the testimonies of administration spokesmen before Congress and sent numerous experts to testify and to speak before prominent citizens' committees.

Kennedy, perhaps, sensed the cost of presenting the treaty as an item in a new context. He therefore related the test ban *to the old context as well,* arguing that the treaty, in effect, was a bit that fitted into the Cold War context. Similarly, the wheat agreement was first introduced as a tension-reducing step but was thereafter increasingly presented as a Cold War measure which would point up Russian agricultural deficiencies. In retrospect, it seems that Kennedy initially underestimated both the costs of changing the public's image and the political risks involved.

The Kennedy project illustrates our conception of *the costs of changing societal knowledge* and the constraints anchoring institutional contexts. These include: (1) psychological forces (i.e., challenging a context generates strains in those who believe in it because of the insecurity and threat contained in a transition); (2) economic vested interests (some industries, unions, and armed services stood to lose with a detente); and (3) political forces—attempting to shift to a new context allows opposition groups to identify with the "same" old context and to charge the innovator with inconsistent and unjustifiable if not treasonable tendencies. We do not suggest, of course, that a contextual transformation was not possible in this situation; our purpose is to highlight what its costs might have been and to illustrate a fallacy in the voluntaristic approach to societal knowledge.[5]

The Influence of Active Publics

Additional research is needed about societal contexts and how they may be changed. Most of the work on public opinion and attitude change is atomistic and voluntaristic—how to change the attitudes of individual persons toward candidates or brands of soap.

A frequent question is, "To what degree do elites and to what degree do "the people" influence events and images?" The "textbook" theory of democracy (still being taught in many schools) holds that elites *represent* the publics. The reaction against this naive theory emphasizes that most of the public has little knowledge about politics, and much of that is molded by the elites. This may be an over-reaction, and we suggest a third approach. Elites are relatively free to set the societal course so long as changes are "bit" changes, or relate to "vague" issues. When, however, elites initiate changes that contravene institutionalized contexts, backlash will be powerful.[6] Consequently, elites must either first change the contexts or avoid contextual (fundamental) changes. Many voters who know little about their congressman will react strongly if he "steps out of line" on a major issue (the southern congressman voting for a civil rights bill). Thus the citizen in a democracy grants the elites their freedom, but not to "rock the boat," not to change contexts.

By allowing the elites and experts this scope—within the contexts set via consensus-building—a pragmatic base for democratic process arises. This very arrangement, of course, can paralyze transformation if the elites fear that any policy change requires a change of context and consequently a difficult course in public education. An active society, however, must confront these constraints.

Here the distinction between active and passive publics is relevant. Various studies report active publics (whose members follow issues closely, work in campaigns, contribute time and/or money, write letters to the editor, and so on) constitute perhaps from 5 to 15 per cent of the voters.[7] If a policy violates the context of an active public, costs to the elite will be high. Members will protest, shift their vote, reduce contributions, and generally exert counter-pressures. The protest of passive publics, contrariwise, takes the form of reduced productivity, less conscientious tax-paying, grumbling, and the like.

Many say that most voters' decisions are more affected by party loyalty and candidates' personalities than by issues. Parties, however, do provide a cognitive and normative context.

When a party violates the voters' contexts, members will shift, as happened in 1964 when many Republicans bolted Goldwater to support Johnson.

Studies are needed to explore systematically the following factors which affect the costs of changing the institutional context: (1) the amount of effort invested in the context's initial introduction, (2) the latent interests it serves, (3) the kinds of reinforcing mechanisms that grow around it (e.g. mass media support), and (4) the length of time it has been reinforced. To establish the Cold War policy, for example, took much effort—more than a single article by George Kennan[8] and a speech to Congress by President Truman. Many other "bit" events piled up in the U.S., as well as the formation of Communist governments in the "Iron Curtain" countries and Soviet intervention in Iran, Turkey, Greece, and especially Czechoslovakia. With all these events, the policy became a *cliché*—thus it is not surprising that President Kennedy could not change it in three months.

Elites *possess a choice* in their strategy of context-shifting. They may introduce new "bits" of information (e.g. reports illustrating the plight of the poor in the U.S.). To reduce the cost, the bits tend to be fitted into the old context (in this case, as minor corrections to weaknesses in a free enterprise economy), in hopes they will accumulate and win acceptance before they are "roofed" with a new context. Elite members—officials, columnists, speakers—contribute bits of information and interpretation. At some point, however, opposition elites may call attention to the "new-context" meaning of the gathering bits, as if to "cry plot." Public resentment may gather and smother the contextual shift.[9]

The alternative strategy is to confront the contextuating orientation directly, without the process of gradual bit-introduction. This strategy requires considerable investment, may backfire, and may involve large risks because of costs noted by the opposition.

Affecting these dynamics is the fact that the contextuating orientation often revolves around a contextuating key *symbol or slogan which absorbs consensus.* Contexts are thus built around Pearl Harbor (sneak attack), Munich (appeasement), or Little Rock (the domestic use of federal force—"bayonets"). New bits are readily absorbed if they fit these symbols. It was argued, for example, that the atomic test ban treaty would be another Munich which exposed the country to a new Pearl Harbor, and that civil rights legislation would bring another Little Rock. Such contextuating symbols have special potency because they arise from shared collective experience and thus support the status quo. On the other hand, when a new experience does force a sudden turn (Pearl Harbor), deep-seated contexts like isolationism give way readily.

Without such striking events, "pseudo-events" are sometimes manufactured. Sit-ins and pray-ins and other confrontation of the early 1960s dramatized the Negro plight. Elites may stage a "national conference," much as commercial interests launch contests among high school students. Public attitudes about such creations could be studied more systematically. A hypothesis in need of exploration: It seems simpler to alter collective images in favor of intergroup *hostility* (war, race conflict), than to induce intergroup *cooperation* (the Atlantic alliance, racial reconciliation).

Costs of Changing Contexts

In short, societal knowledge is much more than a set of images in individual minds. It has social, economic, and political foundations; and both societal learning and unlearning involve a complex process of institutional change which—like other such processes—is in part ongoing but in part *guided.*

Our purpose here has been to illustrate the conditions under which societal knowledge may be revised. Elites are like drivers who keep their eyes on the road and change their direction as they see its turns. The passengers (publics) maintain a more contextuating view of the road and the driving and may call a halt if there is too much veering. The drivers, anticipating this possibility, use information campaigns in the attempt to *change the contexts* governing the passengers' perspectives. We have sought to define the issues in the process: the effects of the elites' actions on the societal knowledge of the members, the ramifications of changes in the members' knowledge for the elites' capacity to guide, and the costs incurred by a "change of course."

NOTES

*Detailed references will be found in *The Active Society*, pp. 168–171.

1. Alex Inkeles and Raymond A. Bauer, *The Soviet Citizen* (Cambridge: Harvard University Press, 1959), Chapter 7.

2. Samuel Lubell, "Sputnik and American Public Opinion," *Columbia University Forum*, Vol. 1 (Winter, 1957), pp. 15–21.

3. Clark Tibbetts (ed.), *Handbook of Social Gerontology* (Chicago: University of Chicago Press, 1960).

4. Amitai Etzioni, "A Psychological Approach to Change," in *Studies In Social Change* (New York: Holt, Rinehart and Winston, 1966), pp. 79–109.

5. Edward A. Shils and Morris Janowitz, "Cohesion and Disintegration in the Wehrmacht in World War II," *Public Opinion Quarterly*, Vol. 12 (1948), pp. 281–315.

6. Wallace S. Sayre and Nelson W. Polsby, "American Political Science and the Study of Urbanization," in Philip M. Hauser and Leo F. Schnore (eds.), *The Study of Urbanization* (New York: Wiley, 1965).

7. V. O. Key, *Public Opinion and American Democracy* (New York: Knopf, 1961).

8. George F. Kennan, "The Sources of Soviet Conduct," *Foreign Affairs*, Vol. 25 (1947), pp. 566–582. This is the famous article advocating "containment" of the Soviet Union.

9. William Kornhauser, *The Politics of Mass Society* (New York: Free Press, 1959), p. 61.

CHAPTER VI

The Criticism of Elite Policies*

We have just discussed the costs of "turning" a whole society in a new direction by revising its societal knowledge. It is now important to ask how the elites come to attempt such a turn in the first place. This chapter will pursue these questions: Who *criticizes* elite policy and suggests turns and changes; how these critics are protected from penalty for daring to criticize "the powers that be"; and what are the relationships in general between those who perform the two functions of knowledge, *the intellectual elites* (whose job is to gather, analyze, and synthesize the information), and the *political elites* (who interpret the knowledge, make the decisions, and issue the action commands).

To place this chapter inside our larger framework: We are still examining the "knowledge" portion of the cybernetic process. The other two cybernetic elements—decision-making and power—are being strongly implied as we proceed. Now if we recognize that in the last chapter we were touching on the idea of consensus formation (in asking how "the people" would react to attempts to change direction), we have introduced all the major independent variables of the theory of societal guidance.

Looking more closely at the command center, its intellectual elites and its political (decision-making) elites, we find a feedback process going on. This is the criticism of the latter by the former. The intellectual elites are not merely criticizing "bits" about the leaders' performance, they are launching at-

Notes for this Chapter are on pages 71 and 72.

tacks on their entire context. This deserves comment. First, we must understand the *perspective* of the group.

The Need for a Guiding Perspective

At any given moment any group—especially its leaders—has a particular world-view of itself and its place in the world—its way of looking at things, its frame of reference. Some call this view a community of assumptions; we will call it the *perspective.* It is composed of a set of ideas and assumptions shared by the elites and active members of a group which sets a context for its view of the world and of itself. Through the lens of this perspective the world is scanned with contextuating eyes. Because of it the elites can agree on agendas and get decisions made: they can operate. Without it, an elite, faced with myriad facts, interpretations, and alternative plans, would be flooded, overloaded, and paralyzed into inaction or split by dissension. It performs the same organizing function for elites as stereotyped attitudes do for individuals, as was noted a half-century ago by Walter Lippmann.[1]

A political party, for example, "sees" a pre-election period in the context of maximum success at the polls; a university's perspective is tripartite: teaching, research, and service; a corporation views its world from the perspective of profit-maximization. All of these groups, of course, also face the *standard* tasks of recruitment, personnel, morale, accounting, change, and survival; and each *sees the same situation*—e.g., a political campaign—through the filter of *its own perspective.*

Only when the perspective prevents relearning long after the reality has changed significantly is a point reached at which the perspective's *costs* outweigh its *gains.* In terms of the two functions of knowledge, the loss in reality-testing outweighs the gains of conflict-reduction, solidarity, and shared group "meaning." More and more spokesmen will agree it's "time for a change."

THE CRITICISM OF ELITE POLICIES

A perspective can be held too tenaciously, to say the least. To show the power of preconceptions about policy, take the example of strategic bombing of Europe in World War II.[2] Allied leaders—military and civilian alike—believed that bombing could destroy the Nazi capability. Shortly after the war, however, the Strategic Bombing Survey conducted a thorough examination. It was found that while strategic bombing had killed at least 300,000 German men, women, and children, it also had killed 155,546 British and American airmen. Damage to enemy production—until the final year of the war—was not great. In fact the bombing of Hamburg diverted several kinds of German civilian activity into war production and its output actually increased. Part of the difficulty was precisely the topic of our present discussion: poor knowledge. Allied "experts" held incorrect information about the German economic and social system, especially an underestimation about slack, conversion, and substitution of facilities and services. The U.S. perspective on bombing hangs on, as shown in Vietnam.

REVISING PERSPECTIVES

Now our point can be made: *Effective units are those whose organization of knowledge permits institutionalized revision of the perspective.* The research behind the Beveridge report fueled Britain's move toward democratization after World War II; a generation of research on genetics as well as prejudice and discrimination preceded the U.S. "civil rights period" following 1954; and study by a small number of educators in the 1880s and 1890s facilitated the move toward graduate programs at Harvard, Yale, Johns Hopkins, and several other leading universities—an important step in the "knowledge revolution" we will discuss in the next chapter.[3]

How does the group or society acquire this critical arm? The organization requires offices whose functions are (1) to remain outside the perspective and to analyze information objectively and (2) to exert pressure on the political elites to change the perspectives as they lose validity.

The fact is that the process by which new orientations enter and become established is not a mechanical, but a socio-political one: people engaging in various kinds of interaction. Ideas *by themselves* have no political power. Rather, the process becomes a conflict between power elites and knowledge-elites who promote alternative perspectives (often in coalition with rival political elites). The intellectuals take on a mobilizing function. The critics must push forward their criticism, out from the ivory tower. Thus it was that the philosophers of the Enlightenment proposed the new image of individual man and free society as "modernization" struck western Europe; that Thomas Hill Green and the Fabian socialists in the 1880s (from different points of view) criticized capitalist laissez-faire and recommended "welfare" policies; that Gandhi and Nehru rallied India against British colonial rule; and that the atomic physicists worked for disarmament and the peaceful use of the atom after Hiroshima and Nagasaki.

Fundamental Criticism of Policy

To remain adaptive, a group or society requires eternal vigilance about its goals and the means taken to pursue them. *Fundamental criticism* is the function of those sub-units whose task is to monitor the reigning perspectives and to challenge them when they near the rigid stage of "formalism," when they become detached from reality. Since such criticism challenges not bits—which can be changed within the existing system—but the context, we refer to it as fundamental criticism. In less crucial situations bit-criticism enhances reality-testing by demonstrating how changes can strengthen the system. But when the community's detachment from reality is large, bit-criticism is dysfunctional because it conceals the disparity and delays overdue change, applying the "band-aid approach" when surgery is indicated.

Two main structural conditions seem necessary for the provision of fundamental criticism. First, the critical sub-units *must operate continually*, even when there is no need or opportunity for the transformation of the perspective. Continued criticism, coming from several quarters, "piles up" and gives legitimacy to the critique, especially because the system most in need of fundamental criticism is likely to be the one most resistant to it and least inclined to transform. And when the perspective needs changing considerable preparation is required *before* breakdown, so that support can be mobilized. The "loyal opposition" within the American Medical Association, composed of 200 outstanding physicians and seeking a change in the Association's position on health insurance, failed to persist in its criticism through the 1950s, so that no change was possible; Medicare came into being only upon continued pressure from diverse groupings.[4]

Second, a value of toleration for such criticism must be a part of the *established* perspective—a tolerance for basically divergent viewpoints. Permissiveness must be written into the by-laws, so to speak. Scientific communities tend to accept this openness to dissent. Several U.S. trade unions maintain independent boards, to give them a critical stance.[5] Within the Republican party the Ripon Society has performed a similar function. It may be no coincidence that ancient Athens tolerated criticism never before seen in history (with of course many exceptions as in the cases of Anaxagoras and Socrates) and also attained new peaks in civilization. Where the system resents criticism the penalties can be harsh, as befell the Chinese Universities which led the anti-Mao dissent of 1968–1969.

THREE SOURCES OF FUNDAMENTAL CRITICISM

The critical function requires one or more sub-units which gain a *special "protection,"* being left immune from social pressure. More, the critics are *rewarded* for their questioning of a supra-unit's basic assumptions. Examples are bureaus charged with R&D, the king's jester or "fool," and to some extent ancient oracles like the one at Delphi.

The question arises: Which sub-units are likely to fulfill

the critical function? The answer varies with the kind of society, but we will consider three types of units.

In pluralistic societies the press was a potential critic, but its performance has been uneven. We know, of course, that much space in the press is devoted to advertising and escapist material (comics, sports, fashions, menus, crime, and sex stories). And the very structure of newsmen's professional norms encourage particularistic rather than institutionalized reporting. The mayor is criticized; the system continues after his defeat. The media tend to stop short of exposing flaws in the working of the institutions—their criticism is not fundamental.

The situation differs for a very small number of newspapers and magazines—the quality press. These allocate more space to information, less to tension-reduction. "Crusading," however, is rare, almost a thing of the past; "muckraking" confers little cachet. A Drew Pearson becomes "controversial," a stigmatizing term. The critical function falls to such periodicals as *The New Republic* and *The Nation*, and the underground press, but their circulation is small, even among intellectuals and elites. The *New York Times* of the later 1960s has assumed an increasingly *interpretive* role, and this stance facilitates criticism.

A second structural foundation for the critical function is national legislatures, yet many feel that a decline has set in.[6] Parliaments seem to exercise their critical function more for domestic than for foreign matters, even in a period when the relevance of foreign affairs is high. While the units which need to be critically reviewed—governmental agencies and corporations, armed services, and school systems—have developed sizeable organs for the collection, synthesis, and promotion of knowledge, legislatures have only very small R&D units. They depend largely on knowledge provided and interpreted for them by either executive or partisan interests. Attempts at encompassing overviews are few and ineffectual, although occasional "white papers" and reports on drugs and organized crime show their potential value. In general, greater investment is required if legislatures are to play a strong critical role.

THE INTELLECTUAL AS SOCIETY'S CRITIC

(While it is difficult to evaluate relative performances, we suggest that in post-modern societies *the unattached intellectuals play a more important critical role than the press, the legislature, and probably both combined.* By "unattached" intellectuals we mean those with no institutional commitment to any elite; they are found especially in the universities but also in autonomous policy-research centers and in a few bohemian quarters. *As contrasted to experts,* they have two attributes: they are concerned with *contextual* matters, while experts are more bit-oriented; and they often deal with evaluative interpretations, while experts are more concerned with reality-testing and cognitive interpretation.[7])

Much fundamental criticism originates with the intellectuals. Examples: Ralph Nader single-handedly challenged the Detroit automobile industry and its safety and construction practices;[8] Michael Harrington dramatized poverty in the U.S.;[9] Lord Keynes suggested a way to fuller employment through government action;[10] John Kenneth Galbraith isolated the starved "public sector" amid the affluent private economy;[11] Lederer and Burdick's *The Ugly American* dramatized the nation's inability to guide the foreign world;[12] a series of intellectuals redefined the status of the mentally ill, criminals, and alcoholics as sick people; and James B. Conant launched a closer look at the U.S. school system.[13] Each of these and many more large critical ideas deserves study of its *path from idea to policy and the modes of overcoming resistance.* The role of the intellectual as critic seems to be growing; certainly the *number* of intellectuals is rising every year.

Structurally, the university "frees" the professor for such work. Not only does he have time to think and write, but tenure allows him the autonomy to make public his ideas without fear of reprisal; he is not "exposed" to sanctions. In pre-modern times less institutionalized settings sufficed, such as coffee houses, patrons' homes, and small magazine shops.[14] Such criticism is characteristically more radical and broad in scope than campus-based work, but less "professional" and scientific. The latter type seems to be more acceptable in post-modern societies. The division of labor between the university and the other centers provides a complementarity, each taking strength from the other. The centers tend to criticize the university and reinforce its critical function.

THE FALLACY OF CONSENSUS AMONG CRITICS

A common fallacy is the suggestion that the critics are ineffective because they arrive at no consensus about what is faulty or what needs to be done. Further, it has been argued that any consensus among intellectuals is merely another untested perspective. We suggest, on the contrary, first, that intellectuals' perspectives are *relatively* more open to innovative interpretation and empirical testing than political ones or those of the public, because of the institutionalization of the value of truth among intellectuals and because the pressure of extrinsic interests is less. (In this connection it must be acknowledged that political elites are held accountable for their positions, while this is much less true of intellectuals.) Secondly, it is not the function of intellectuals to achieve consensus. That is the function of *the entire political process.* The intellectuals' role is to pry open the walls within which the society boxes itself and to suggest ways out; *which way out is to be decided by the community as a whole.* Intellectuals cannot guarantee which action programs have what per cent of probable success, although they can provide rough "*cost*" estimates. What they can do is to enrich the debate. Consensus among them is not necessary.

RELATIONSHIPS BETWEEN CRITICS AND ACTIVES

Relationships among the three kinds of elites—political, expert, and intellectual—will affect the quality of both the reality-testing and the fundamental criticism needed in an active society. Each of the three may poach to some extent on the other two territories, but there is a tendency toward specialization. Limited segregation between them is most evident in pre-modern societies in which the ruler performed all three functions with some staff aid. Underdeveloped nations usually suffer from weakness at the empirical level; ideas travel readily from the intellectual to the political elite without sufficient expert screening and testing. Even in post-modern societies some interpenetration will be found, as when intellectuals become co-opted by or actually share in the margins of power; the extent to which they become mandarins or "yes-men" is an empirical question. In comparison to earlier societies, which suffered from considerable political penetration into the expert realm, post-modern societies often suffer from a lack of political guidance from experts (especially in the relations between civilian political elites and military experts). Oddly enough, the active society requires the reassertion of the primacy of political guidance over the experts' view of the world.

The three kinds of elites are affected, of course, by public opinion. The deliberations of the political elites are scanned and evaluated by the active publics, and accepted or rejected. The opinions of the publics—as expressed in opinion polls, the media, and conversation—also affect the degree to which there is tolerance for the intellectuals and their criticism, respect for experts, and support for political elites.

Criticism against political elites can take two paths. One is direct, from the intellectuals to the elites. The other is indirect, consisting of appeals to the publics and to the opposition—i.e., attempts to transform public outlooks and to mobilize "grass roots" support to force a change in the perspective of the political elites. Societies can be compared as to their relative reliance on the two channels. The two are not mutually exclusive, of course; progress in one is often related to progress in the other. Elites pay attention to "best-seller" book lists, and the public is sometimes told what books the President is reading. Harrington's book on poverty, for example, spurted in sales after it became known that President Kennedy had read it with interest.

Interpenetration Between the Elites

A popular theory holds that policy makers should remain segregated from the collectors and assessors of intelligence; the policy maker should interpret the information and make his decision.[15]

This widely-held model is weak on two counts: it focuses on basic research, while in fact more "applied" than "basic" research is involved; and experts play a far more important (and complex) role in recasting information than the model implies.

Most of the information used by post-modern societies is "applied," and only indirectly based on basic research. If federal obligations are taken as a rough indicator, the U.S. committed $1,689.9 millions in 1965 to basic research and $12,909.7 millions to applied research and development.[16] This applied information is gathered by engineers, x-ray technicians, social workers, and so on, not scientists. A considerable degree of control inflicts surprisingly little damage on their work. Applied research has been carried out quite effectively even in totalitarian countries.[17] Political intervention in such work, even in Stalin's day, may be less stringent than was once believed but can be much greater than the amounts which the segregation model assumes that research can tolerate.[18]

Second, as custodians of reality testing, the information experts play a more important role in recasting political information than the segregation model suggests.[19] The decision-making process is much more complex, permitting numerous information-influence mechanisms to operate prior to the final decision.

Experts can be found to support almost any side in most political contests through their reports or through testimony before executive or legislative committees. This is done sometimes by drawing on different sets of facts, but much more commonly *by supplying particular interpretations to available facts.* Conflicting interpretations about the danger of nuclear fallout, the probabilities of surviving a nuclear attack, and the effects of Medicare or of violence in the mass media are examples.[20] The Armed Services organize advisory corporations, whose studies support and sometimes even extend the perspectives of the services, even though they may differ about details.[21] Industries maintain public relations divisions to magnify and interpret "their" experts' findings on cancer and tobacco, vitamins and growth, drugs and pregnancy. Whether they cite "pure" or "applied" research, the motif is "best foot forward." Even outside the commercial domain, experts may "psych out" the prejudices of their several directors and present materials which, while legitimate in themselves, are difficult for hostile directors to counter, thus assuring serious consideration of the experts' viewpoint. Thus the effectiveness of experts, somewhat like that of attorneys, is determined not only by evidence but by *the skill employed in presenting it.*[22] It is not that experts strive to hoodwink people; the entire decision process is as complex as the issues, so that even an unbiased and expertly trained judge could not readily decide on the basis of information alone. Even the sagest of men sometimes admit that they "agree with both sides."

In practice, the differences between "right" and "wrong" approaches are unclear but are usually a matter of being more or less *effective*—and under conditions which may have developed *after* the hearing. The tests of the relative effectiveness of such matters as foreign aid, civil rights legislation, or police codes are, as a rule, difficult to establish, ambiguous, and open to different expert interpretations.[23] Further, because of the high cost of expertise, political elites defend "their" experts from being discredited. We do not argue that uninformed men are the counsellors while the wise go unheeded. We simply submit that *the selection of experts and their performance on the job make up a complex, partly evaluative and partly political process.*

Competition in Knowledge-Seeking Through Pluralism

What, then, can lead to a more effective societal organization of knowledge input? The prevailing answer posits *pluralism* both in production and in input. If one elite (or school of thought) gains a monopoly of either production or access to an elite, the actor's reality testing will become less effective. A more effective course will be pursued when *several* knowledge producers have access to elites. This must remain, of course, a matter of degree; our discussion above has indicated that considerable politicization of knowledge-supply and decision-making will obtain even with pluralism.

Further, it appears that a measure of competition is healthy in knowledge production. A scientist who is refused support from one agency could always turn to another. The proposal to establish a cabinet-level U.S. Department of Science has not received wide approval because it would concentrate the sources of support for research.[24] This applies to intra-organizational production of knowledge as well. One of the arguments for intelligence collection by the three Armed Forces, the CIA, the State Department, and other agencies is that pluralism is thereby fostered. In cities where one publisher owns both the morning and the afternoon newspapers, news staffs often attempt to maintain autonomy and competition, for much the same reasons.

With competing agencies comes the question of financial support to each. While a single brilliant mind may generate a great idea, under most conditions there is a positive association between investment of funds and talent and the quality of knowledge produced. Given a certain level of resources, pluralism and an active orientation require that the several units be given appropriate funding. Otherwise the knowledge contest resembles a court fight between a battery of corporation lawyers and a young night school graduate from the Legal Aid Society. This permits due consideration of ideas which have no immediate appeal and little power.

The open society also allows for *protective anticipation:* Deprived minorities may be heard long before they command sufficient power to force attention by confronting headquarters (HQ) or possibly producing violence. An equalitarian allocation of knowledge units allows for an awareness of gathering clouds on the horizon before the storm topples the gates.

A new role—that of "the advocate" in ghetto areas, introduced in the late 1960s—has marked a gain, by providing research skills to spotlight grievances. The new knowledge is vital to reform, although all too frequently a show of force is also required, as the consensus-formation process falters on its upward course to HQ. Thus while elites need knowledge to keep the shop running, heretofore "blind" groups need it to win a greater share of the pie.

The function of pluralism in knowledge-production is clear. We would add another prerequisite for the active society: Systematic provision for the three filters—intellectual, expert, and political—and for their articulation with each other and with the active publics. A society that is free to test its ideas and to experiment with new ones cannot restrict itself to the filter—the perspective—of the elites in power; this society must provide for continuing fundamental criticism from several sources and remain open to it. The self-critical society—active in its use of societal knowledge—cannot be brought about unless the post-modern society is transformed by a fuller exercise of the critical function. John Gardner's apt term for the group that can crush freedom and diversity is "the amiable majority."[26]

NOTES

*Detailed references will be found in *The Active Society*, pp. 190–196.

1. Walter Lippmann, *Public Opinion* (New York: Macmillan, 1922), Part 3.

2. Harold L. Wilensky, *Organizational Intelligence* (New York: Basic Books, 1967).

3. Christopher Jencks and David Riesman, *The Academic Revolution* (Garden City: Doubleday, 1968), pp. 13, 260.

4. "The American Medical Association: Power, Purpose and Politics in Organized Medicine," *Yale Law Journal*, Vol. 63 (May, 1954), pp. 938–1022, esp. 1007–1018.

5. Wilensky, *op. cit.*, p. 170.

6. Philip Donham and Robert Fahey, *Congress Needs Help* (New York: Random House, 1966).

7. Raymond Aron, *The Opium of the Intellectuals* (Garden City: Doubleday, 1957).

8. Ralph Nader, *Unsafe at Any Speed* (New York: Grossman, 1965).

9. Michael Harrington, *The Other America* (New York: Macmillan, 1962).

10. John Maynard Keynes, *The General Theory of Employment, Interest and Money* (London: Macmillan, 1936).

11. John Kenneth Galbraith, *The Affluent Society* (Boston: Houghton-Mifflin, 1958).

12. William J. Lederer and Eugene Burdick, *The Ugly American* (New York: Norton, 1958).

13. James B. Conant, *The American High School Today* (New York: McGraw-Hill, 1959).

14. Lewis A. Coser, *Men of Ideas* (New York: Free Press, 1965).

15. Don K. Price, *The Scientific Estate* (Cambridge: Harvard University Press, 1965).

16. National Science Foundation, *Federal Funds for Research, Development, and Other Scientific Activities: Fiscal Years 1965, 1966 and 1967*, Vol. 15 (Washington: Government Printing Office, 1966), p. 77.

17. Leo Orleans, "Research and Development in Communist China," *Science*, Vol. 157 (July 28, 1967), pp. 392–400.

18. Bernard Barber, *Science and the Social Order* (New York: Collier, 1962), pp. 115–120.

19. Don K. Price, *Government and Science* (New York: New York University Press, 1954), pp. 134 ff.; Ralph E. Lapp, *The New Priesthood* (New York: Harper and Row, 1965).

20. Compare Herman Kahn, *On Thermonuclear War* (Princeton: Princeton University Press, 1961) and Robert Dentler and Phillips Cutright, *Hostage America* (Boston: Beacon Press, 1963), pp. 1–76. Also, Otto N. Larsen, *Violence and the Mass Media* (New York: Harper and Row, 1968).

21. For a study which reveals the inadequacy of the segregation model, see Bruce L. R. Smith, "Strategic Expertise and National Security Policy," in John D. Montgomery and Arthur Smithies (eds.), *Public Policy*, Vol. 13 (1964), pp. 69–106.

22. Lawrence Cranberg, "Ethical Problems of Scientists," *The Educational Record*, Vol. 46 (1965).

23. Albert D. Biderman, "Social Indicators and Goals," in Raymond A. Bauer (ed.), *Social Indicators* (Cambridge: M.I.T. Press, 1966), pp. 68–153.

24. Wallace S. Sayre, "Scientists and American Science Policy," in Robert Gilpin and Christopher Wright (eds.), *Scientists and National Policy-making* (New York: Columbia University Press, 1964), pp. 105–106.

25. See the discussion by Frances Fox Piven and others on advocacy planning in *Social Policy*, Vol. 1 (July–August, 1970), pp. 33–41.

26. John Gardner, *Self-Renewal: The Individual and the Innovative Society* (New York: Harper and Row, 1963), p. 71.

CHAPTER VII

The Increasing Symbolization of Society*

In the modern period and at an accelerating rate in the post-modern, *symbols have become increasingly important,* while the relative importance of objects has declined. Since symbolic elements are more malleable than objects, the greater their role in society, the more readily can that society be recast. As society becomes less monolithic, it gains potential to guide itself.

The evidence comes from several sectors. Education is expanding virtually everywhere in the world. More occupations call for symbolic efforts than for manual efforts. By 1958 the U.S. became the first society in which more than half the labor force worked in the tertiary (services) sector while less than half was employed in mining, agriculture, and manufacturing. Knowledge has, of course, modernized the farm: One farm worker supplied 10 persons in 1930—and about 40 in 1970.[1] Other modern societies show similar shifts.

The Knowledge Industry

Only recently has one portion of the service sector become recognized as "The Knowledge Industry." This includes not only education but communications (printing, broadcasting, and other forms of organized dissemination of symbols) and research and development. One economist has estimated that the total

Notes for this Chapter are on pages 80 and 81.

expenditure for knowledge in the U.S. in 1958 was an incredible *29 per cent of the GNP*, and was growing.[2]

Educational leaders assume greater importance in public issues. With the bursting social problems of the 1960s and 1970s, governments feel required to call on experts for advice on commissions studying poverty, the birth rate, crime, race, drugs, the mass media, education and many other problems. Professors who once entertained undergraduates at afternoon tea find themselves testifying in Washington. Their knowledge, both broader and deeper and less self-interested than that of bureaucrats, is often politically controversial but tends to save headaches later on by permitting more intelligent planning. Again, knowledge can forestall ill-conceived programs.

In the military sector, a sharp rise in the use of symbols occurred with the strategic arms race among the superpowers, and not merely in terms of quantitative production. A major shift has also developed in qualitative terms, such as the speed at which a country is able to shift from old to new models (e.g., from fluid to solid propellant missiles). Such recasting requires R&D. Total U.S. expenditure for R&D rose from $1.5 billion in 1945 to an estimated $17.3 billion in 1963.[3]

The investment in knowledge has grown similarly, both in absolute figures and as a percentage of GNP. Between 1960 and 1965, the U.S. government spent considerably more on R&D than on three other "permanent" sectors combined—subsidies to farmers, support to veterans, and foreign aid. Similarly, knowledge expands in the health field. In the post-modern period, the number of research M.D.'s has grown more rapidly than the number of M.D. practitioners. Trends in the U.S.S.R. and other nations move in the same direction.[4]

The Increasing Importance of Education in Stratification

Another reason that society is becoming more symbolic is that the bases of stratification are becoming more symbolic and therefore more malleable; *the importance of education as a criterion of class level increases* while the economic factor declines.[5] The "product of education" is individuals with changed symbolic capacities and changed values. Material facilities are certainly needed for schools, but they are relatively unimportant as compared to the interaction of students and faculty, ideas, and all educational media.

It is quite true that the aims of education and the techniques and organization to accomplish those aims—whatever these be for given branches of learning—are today subject to unending (and doubtless healthy) controversy. Thus the actual contributions of education are often unexpected and subject to debate. Should we focus on liberal education or specialized training? Must courses be made more "relevant" to the student? Relevant in what sense? Meantime more people, young and old, and especially in the lower socio-economic classes, are in school for more courses and for more years.

As a consequence of greater symbolization, there appears a shift from education as a reflection of economic relationships *to education as a determinant of these relationships.*[6] Two decades ago the individual's social status was more determined by financial standing and by ethnic origins. Since that time teachers and professors have gained in prestige, and education is more readily taken as an access road to elites. Societal guidance has speeded this shift through more egalitarian allocations of resources among units and through creating more opportunity structures for the underprivileged as seen in fellowships, scholarships, loans, special recruitment efforts, poverty assistance programs (Head Start, Upward Bound, Job Corps), military educational facilities, and the like.[7] Thus education is increasingly a major avenue and criterion of upward mobility, although the "meritocracy" point has certainly not yet been reached at which the non-college-educated becomes the lower class, the college-educated the middle class, and holders of higher degrees the upper class.[8]

Knowledge as a Spur to the Economy

If knowledge is a transforming force in society, at what points does it exert the greatest propellant thrust? Some years ago economists were stressing material forces—capital formation and the development of specific industries—as a "take-off" base for economic development. More recent is the focus on the *investment in "human" capital,* in education and training.[9]

For developed nations, there is a growing recognition of the power of R&D. Many economists, especially of the left, predicted that capitalism would die of overcapacity.[10] Ability to produce would outgrow demand, bringing unemployment and economic collapse. This, of course, has failed to happen. Accordingly, increasing stress was placed on the role of innovation, finding new products and services and promotional devices to create new demands. For a time it was held that "prosperity depends on investment, investment on technology, and technology on science. Ergo, prosperity depends on science." [11] But it has recently become evident that special conditions must be met if the knowledge industry is to pace development. In England between 1958 and 1963, for example, R&D expenditures rose by almost 60 per cent, but the economy grew at a much slower pace. A similar finding was made for the U.S.[12]

The best available explanation for this relatively small secondary-priming effect is the heavy concentration of R&D in Britain and the U.S. in *one sector: Military and space R&D.* These activities absorbed 89 per cent of the R&D appropriations of $14.8 billion in the U.S. for the fiscal year 1965.[13] The very limited "spill-over" into other sectors of the economy suggest that barriers exist around military and space R&D which are much greater than with such work in medical, social, and civilian research. The extension and application of civilian R&D does not face the problems posed in the military realm—secrecy and classified information, esoteric products (war and space products do not convert readily into household use), and snags with property rights and legislative requirements.

Much more leverage is applied by that R&D which is

linked to the rest of society, such as medical, educational, consumer, and social research. Fewer difficulties attend the conversion: New drugs call for new equipment and new marketing procedures; new findings about learning bring on new educational technologies and spur new efforts at preparing lower-class youth for more education, thus creating a new cycle of demand for education and launching a new class-generation into the post-modern period. Western European societies, putting their R&D into civilian channels in the 1950s and early 1960s, showed higher economic growth rates than the U.S. or England.[14] Thus it appears that "investment in knowledge" is best applied to those more closely related knowledge sectors, to propel a national economy. It is profitable to recall that the Puritan ideas of Calvin, as Max Weber's classic thesis tells us, reached precisely those men who were ready to "take off" in bold new capitalistic enterprises.

The Unequal Distribution of Knowledge

The knowledge we are discussing—all the education, research, analysis, dissemination, and the facilities to promote these activities—is clearly not spread evenly through all sectors of society. Rather, it "piles up" around elites. Further, the inequality in the *distribution* of knowledge is greater than with many other assets, especially utilitarian ones. A group with good knowledge can compete in a most advantageous way and can also count on increasing its share of knowledge in the future. Inequality in knowledge grows continually, whether we are comparing societies (developed vs. developing), groups (with greater and lesser access to knowledge), sectors (military-industrial as against small business), or regions (50 per cent of R&D expenditures are concentrated in three states—California, New York, and Massachusetts).[15] There are concentrated "centers" of knowledge in each field. Among 79 of the most prominent university departments of sociology in the U.S., for example, the faculty in the top five produced just over 30 per cent of the major sociological publications between 1960 and 1965.[16] The same five (Berkeley, Harvard, Chicago, Michigan, and Columbia) probably produced about one fourth of the publications from the several hundred sociology departments in the country.

Guiding the Application of Knowledge

The key question, in all probability, in societal guidance as applied to knowledge is: To what degree does a society command the capacity to *reassign* knowledge resources? Put another way: Can the distribution of knowledge resources be made responsive to national goals and needs?

The problem resides not so much in controlling the production of knowledge nor in the skewed distribution of knowledge resources but in *the antisocial application of some of these resources.* An illustrating question, to show the direction we will take, is: Should a society permit the marketing of insufficiently-tested drugs?[17] Consequences of the thalidomide case (as in Germany) suggest the significance of the issue.

Historically, the idea of the *national* guidance of the production and use of knowledge was alien to the Western tradition. Laissez-faire policies went unchallenged. Until the modern period, men assumed that *society must adjust to the implications of new knowledge.* This was true even of one of the great encompassing changes of all history, the Industrial Revolution, which "changed everything" about political and economic institutions. Both benefits and costs followed but fundamentally, given the low capacity for societal knowledge then prevailing, nobody had much choice in promoting or resisting the Industrial Revolution. No individual or group "decided" to accept the Industrial Revolution; it just happened. Even today most societies simply adapt to changes, technological and otherwise; they still play a passive role in change.

Societal guidance capacities have come a long way since the 18th century, yet no society has made systematic efforts to amplify and utilize the available cybernetic strategies. The American and British governments set out to develop atomic and thermonuclear weapons with only rudimentary estimates of their international implications and without public knowledge and consent;[18] the military-industrial complex maintains its course in a similar way; pharmaceutical scandals still occur; scientists are exploring chemical means of controlling human behavior.

Few critics seek regulation of the *production* of knowledge; academic freedom and the freedom of the scientist to pursue his hunches are cherished traditions. Few also recognize that in post-modern societies this production is already more nationally guided than the rest of the economy. Federal control is either direct (intramural or "in-house" research) or involves a high degree of specification of the product and the budget, and only rarely is there the "finance without strings" prescribed by the ideological model. The infrequency of "stifling effects" in knowledge production follows from the fact that much of this research is applied and can be closely supervised without threatening the freedom of science. This is generally the practice in consumer industry, in much government-funded work, and in many state universities, acting as "service stations." New guidance mechanisms take the form of congressional committees specializing in "science," the Office of Science and Technology in the White House, and councils of national academies and professional and disciplinary associations; all of these maintain watchdog and control committees.

These remarks hold for societies of quite different persuasions. Communist nations as well as pluralist ones similarly succumb to the mass-use of water-polluting detergents, unsafe cars, and the mass production of cigarettes. In the Soviet Union concentration of educational facilities contravenes societal goals, but attempts to redistribute them have been only partially successful.[19] Thus overcontrol in some areas (e.g. research in genetics) accompanies deficient control elsewhere. Thus it is not merely the related ideologies of capitalism and laissez-faire that can be blamed for these dubious effects of symbolization-and-technology; distortions arise from deeper societal sources. We seek to stress that the capacity for the societal guidance of the use of knowledge is one central factor, and it is tantalizingly low in societies that differ markedly in their political institutions.

What seems needed is greater legitimation of, and investment in, societal guidance over the *application* of knowledge. The *use of property* is subject to regulation in all societies, and knowledge can claim many of the characteristics of property. Since the time of Adam Smith and the heyday of robber-baron capitalism, laissez-faire has virtually disappeared with respect to national intervention in economic activity, and similar guidance over the uses of knowledge seems required in the active society. The problem is not only a lack of guidance per se but also deficient legitimation of the societal guidance of knowledge; a paucity of means and resources; the over-pluralistic, under-centralized nature of guidance systems; and the lack of an anticipatory and therefore preventive guidance system. At present most such mechanisms defer review until *after* the technology has been introduced, thus making "recall" much more costly, if not impossible. After all, the refusal to guide is also a willed act. Just as recent years have witnessed large new investments in education and R&D, new programs of investment in the ability to ascertain the consequences of new knowledge will characterize the active society. Closer relationships between knowledge-relevant groups may thus *protect the less-knowledgeable while spurring innovation in knowledge* directed at the accomplishment of widely shared societal goals.

NOTES

*Detailed references will be found in *The Active Society*, pp. 214–222.

1. Raymond W. Mack, *Transforming America* (New York: Random House, 1967), p. 8.

2. Fritz Machlup, *The Production and Distribution of Knowledge in the U.S.* (Princeton: Princeton University Press, 1962).

3. The 1945 figure is taken from U.S. Bureau of the Census, *Statistical Abstract of the United States: 1957*, p. 495; the 1963 figure is taken from *Reviews of Data on Science Resources*, Vol. 1, No. 4 (Washington, D.C.: National Science Foundation, 1965), p. 6.

4. Alexander Korol, *Soviet Research and Development* (Cambridge: MIT Press, 1965).

5. Comparable studies of the prestige of U.S. occupations for 1947 and 1963 showed that scientists, professors, and school teachers all showed some gains during the period. Robert W. Hodge, Paul M. Siegel, and Peter H. Rossi, "Occupational Prestige in the United States, 1925–1963," *American Journal of Sociology*, Vol. 70 (November, 1964), pp. 286–302. Contrasted to the 1960s, intellectuals held a relatively low position in the early 1950s; see Wilson Record, "The American Intellectual as Black Sheep and Red Rover," *Bulletin of the American Association of University Professors*, Vol. 40 (Winter, 1954–55), pp. 536–554.

6. Jean Floud and A. H. Halsey, "Introduction," to Halsey, Floud, and Anderson (eds.), *Education, Economy and Society* (New York: Free Press, 1961).

7. That the class and racial differential is still great can be seen from many studies. Robert Perucci, "Education, Stratification and Mobility," in Donald A. Hansen and Joel E. Gerstl (eds.), *On Education—Sociological Perspectives* (New York: Wiley, 1967), Chap. 4.

8. Michael Young, *The Rise of the Meritocracy*, 1870–2033 (New York: Random House, 1958).

9. Theodore Schultz, "Investment in Education," in Halsey, Floud, and Anderson, *op. cit.*, pp. 50–52.

10. Joseph A. Schumpeter, *Socialism, Capitalism and Democracy* (New York: Harper & Row, 1947).

11. *London Economist*, October 5, 1963.

12. Robert A. Solo, "Gearing Military R&D to Economic Growth," *Harvard Business Review*, Vol. 40 (Nov.–Dec., 1962), pp. 49–60.

13. National Science Foundation, *Federal Funds for Research, Development and Other Scientific Activities, Fiscal Years 1965, 1966 and 1967, op. cit.*, p. 152.

14. Bruce M. Russet et al., *World Handbook of Political and Social Indicators* (New Haven: Yale University Press, 1964), p. 155.

15. U.S. Census Bureau, *Statistical Abstract of the United States: 1966*, p. 546.

16. Dean D. Knudsen and Ted R. Vaughan, "Quality in Graduate Education," *American Sociologist*, Vol. 4 (February, 1969), pp. 12–19.

17. See, e.g., William M. O'Brien, "Drug Testing," *Bulletin of the Atomic Scientists*, Vol. 25 (January, 1969), pp. 8–14; and Richard Harris, *The Real Voice* (New York: Macmillan, 1964).

18. Warner R. Schilling, "The H-Bomb Decision: How to Decide Without Actually Choosing," *Political Science Quarterly*, Vol. 76 (1961), pp. 24–46.

19. Nicholas DeWitt, *Education and Professional Employment in the USSR*, National Science Foundation, 1961.

CHAPTER VIII

Societal Consciousness and Social Action*

Just as the man who is more aware of his environment is more "active," so it is for groups and societies. The active society will be more aware or "conscious" of itself and the world around it than other societies. This consciousness is in part the perspective of its members—what they hear, read, and talk about; and in part the institutionalization of awareness *in its control centers*—such as adding a "country desk" (e.g., Ghana) in the State Department, publishing a White Paper, holding a Congressional hearing, or installing a new computer and analyzing its data. Consciousness (or awareness—the two terms are used here as synonyms) is a prerequisite of an active unit, one which is self-reviewing and self-correcting in order to be self-guiding. *Consciousness is thus another crucial entity in the active society, like power and knowledge.* A "blind" group can achieve its goals only by luck or charity. A chronic complaint of Marxist leaders (and of leaders of many other aspiring groups) is that their members lack "consciousness."

The issues to be raised in this chapter are: Under what conditions does societal consciousness develop? What are the dynamic relations among its components? And, how does societal consciousness affect social action?

In our use of the term, knowledge can be invalid; *consciousness* can be limited, misdirected, or unfocused—but *not false.* Societal consciousness is an expression of the level, extent, and "topics" of attention and curiosity rather than specific information. At the same time, consciousness and knowledge are obviously closely related; the former focuses the latter. One

 Notes for this Chapter are on pages 89 and 90.

other point: the term is used without the metaphysical assumption of some vague "group mind"; clearly no such entity exists.

Members of a unit may come to share awareness of practically anything, from an abandoned child to a war. *Activation is facilitated when members share consciousness and know it.* That is, they all focus attention not on many different targets, but on the same one or two, like an audience in a theater. They realize what they are doing; they have low "pluralistic ignorance."[1] Also important for an active orientation is that members arrange their awareness in context rather than having a bit of interest here and a bit there. Thus such a combination of bits as linking dollars spent per year for white as against Negro children with a decrease in some Negro children's I.Q.'s as they finish high school can fit into and expand a context, and can become a more potent signal for action. The manner of building these contexts is a topic for further research.

Actions to Increase Consciousness

One major way to increase societal consciousness is for the unit to act collectively. This proposition may seem to run backwards, as in the James-Lange theory. For example, a worker does not join a labor union because he is class-conscious, but he develops class-consciousness by participating in union affairs. The "*project*" is a major type of collective action; this will be discussed extensively in Chapters 13 and 19.

Two other types of collective action are confrontations and "intimate rejections." *Confrontations* (for example, with the police) serve to *involve* the members as well as the elites, and they provide intensive shared experiences that knit the group through the formation of negative counter-symbols, as with the Boston Tea Party, the Haymarket riot, army combat units, and many student movements since Berkeley in 1964. In addition, confrontations exert a multiplier effect by increasing the number and activity of the "activation agents," members who then rally their friends to the movement. More leaders emerge from previously passive quarters, to join with the elites in mobilization.

"Intimate rejection" may also produce a sudden increase in group consciousness. When rejection is encountered in the context of intimate contact, after some measure of equality has been experienced, greater alienating effects are felt by the rising group because the host is now more of a "significant other." Theodore Hertzl, leader of the Zionist movement, was well accepted as a reporter in non-Jewish circles. During the Dreyfus trial in France—a trial in which anti-semitism in the army was crucial—he felt rejected, and this experience galvanized his Zionist activity.[2] Africans who studied in Britain and France tried to deal with intimate rejection by collectivizing their experiences, resulting in a higher level of consciousness of membership in their native groups, a consciousness which they carried with them on their return to their homelands.

Foci of Attention of Active Publics

The political and intellectual elites, as we often note, are key actors in the building of consciousness, consensus, and activation. The extent to which they are supported by active publics and their growing consciousness is likewise vital. The more passive bulk of the group usually lags behind, to be mobilized—if at all—only in crisis. Usually, however, the elites must gain the legitimation and support of the non-elites. This is accomplished most effectively when the elites are responsive to the interests of the members and when consensus-formation reveals to the elites what these interests are. These are important levers of change.

In this historical view, the rise of the several fields of knowledge has followed a certain sequence. Interest in the natural sciences came first, in the social sciences later, and the study of societal guidance is only now emerging. Consciousness of guidance mechanisms has had to wait for the development of the first two kinds of studies. With it, we see greater attention now paid to political consciousness, an awareness of power relations—where the political levers are, what the distribution of power is, and the ways and means by which change is possible. When this interest is high, *together with* a strong command of utilitarian assets, the potential for activation rises. Further, to some degree the two substitute for each other. For instance, efforts to organize the poor, to increase their self-confidence, and to build some collective political awareness (e.g., by instructing them in the workings of City Hall) will increase the action capacity of the poor *before* they gain new resources.[3]

Study can be directed to the *foci of attention* of any relevant unit. For instance, the Republican party pays more attention to the radical left than to the radical right; India has been more concerned, until recently, with industrialization than with the modernization of agriculture. Any group can devote attention to several topics at any time, through a staff division of labor, but we suggest that there is a limit to the number of issues which can receive high priority. Staffs can be expanded, but studies show that the range of effective supervision is limited.[4] The political consequences of an error at lower levels are considerable, hence top decision-makers are obliged to inform themselves of the details to some degree.[5] Groups, in general, can be greatly aware of only a few topics at a time. Rising levels of education, however, may gradually boost this limitation on change; most individuals apparently can absorb more knowledge than they have been getting.[6] This is true person by person, and even more so collectively. When a group rewards learning and consciousness, these symbolic activities can show great increments.

Consciousness and Activeness

This cautionary comment is now in order: there is no

necessary relationship between the level of consciousness and activeness, and this is true for two reasons. First, other factors (e.g., overwhelming power held by elites, or poor knowledge among the "conscious" but unlettered hopefuls) may inhibit high activity levels; second, an increase in consciousness may rather encourage a more reflective, passive orientation. When consciousness is high but commitment is low, we expect the societal equivalent of "I don't give a damn" sometimes found in decadent periods (Rome in its locality-bound third century or France in the pre-Revolution era). The Jewish community in medieval Europe was highly self-conscious, but weak and fairly passive.[7]

When consciousness is high but knowledge is low, people may feel unable to cope with problems. The 1966 U.S. Senate hearings on LSD, for example, revealed much attention focused on the problem but little certainty about what to do. When consciousness is high but power is low, we expect a sense of frustration and helplessness, familiar to reform movements during societal doldrums. Thus the level of consciousness and activation may be quite uneven.

Enlarged awareness fueled gains made by ghetto groups in the 1960s. Poverty leaders in New York went into action when they learned from Richard Cloward and his associates about little-known facts of welfare policy: that the U.S. spends 0.7 per cent of its income for welfare but that the rate is falling; that welfare recipients receive only a fraction of what they are legally entitled to; that traditional welfare and agricultural policies contributed importantly to the farm-to-city migration of millions of Negroes during the 1950s and 1960s.[8] Similar awareness initiated mobilization in many other places—Milwaukee, Chicago, Syracuse, Appalachia—and resulted in such modest gains as improved police protection and welfare services, better tenant leases, the reduction of illegitimate retail business practices, new roads, stoplights at school crossings, and so on.[9] Indeed, consciousness resulting from the diffusion of knowledge about flaws in the workings of social institutions is basic to progressive change. The work of Dickens, Lincoln

Steffens, Upton Sincliar, Rachel Carson, David Brower, and Michael Harrington suggests the range of this factor.

We expect the more conscious individuals or groups to be more creative, because they are more reflective, take more factors into account, and see the wider context—i.e., are aware of more options. They will engage in less trial-and-error behavior, being better prepared to design a more systematic course of action.

"Unlocking" Old Patterns

There are two main links between the level of societal consciousness and the societal capacity for innovation and transformation. One concerns the building of new structures and systems; the other entails the "unlocking" of old ones. Since the first is the province of the intellectual and political elites whose training allows them to design new programs and structures, we will deal only with the second. To unlock an old pattern means that considerable *pressure* must be placed on it, usually in the form of *well-documented criticism* which reaches significant publics. This focusing of public attention can bring change only so long as the issue can be kept "in the public eye." Organizations have done this, especially when they can stimulate "running news stories" on topics like public health and safety. Examples include the Anti-Saloon League and the WCTU with respect to the manufacture and sale of liquor, the Foundation for Infantile Paralysis and polio, and SANE (Committee for a Sane Nuclear Policy).

Less well-organized but ingenious groupings such as college students "manufactured" publicity by various demonstrations to dramatize their opposition to the Vietnam war starting in 1964; the resulting public consciousness "prepared" public opinion to oppose the war when military reverses in 1968 revealed that the war was far from being "won," and national policy shifted toward peace moves. The campaign led by Ralph

Nader, also starting in 1964, to spotlight unsafe automobiles was able to "hold on" long enough to bring about congressional hearings and legislation imposing auto safety standards. The extent to which these standards will be actually imposed, diluted, or strengthened by further legislation depends, in part, on the degree to which the problem commands continued public attention. On the issue of limiting the sale of guns, the assassination of President Kennedy was followed by sharply increased public scrutiny, but attention lagged, and a mild law was passed only after a second wave of spotlighting was prompted by the assassinations of Martin Luther King and Senator Robert Kennedy.[10]

What issues the attentive publics do focus on, for how long and how often, is affected by political leaders, intellectuals, "white papers," hearings, the mass media, and the campaigns of interest groups. If spotlighting is able to dramatize the issue so that it captures public consciousness—and if the vested interest is unable to counter the campaign with persuasive appeals—a wedge is driven into the structure under attack. A few structures disintegrate after one exposure, some change only after repeated exposures, and others are altered only slightly. The move for public health insurance in the U.S. required almost three decades before a change came about, and even then the coverage applied only to the elderly. Thus bit reforms are more likely than fundamental changes.

Another concept, that of *recommitting*, links the two activities of "unlocking" an old structure and of setting a new pattern and course. This notion refers to the society's capacity to "change its mind" and cut back an ongoing program. Totalitarian countries can recommit more readily than pluralistic ones, as in the case of the Soviet Union, which could discontinue its space program with less difficulty than the U.S.

We have to ask the question: Does increased societal consciousness increase the capacity to recommit? Or are the forces that impede transformability—the "stiffness" of bureaucracy and the institutionalization of vested interests—greater than those energizing the attentive publics? When the conserving forces concede, are the concessions only temporary and "token," or can public attention be maintained long enough to bring about significant recommitments?

One factor that may favor such shifts is the degree to which the larger environment is changing. Changing environments favor flexible orientations, including reviewing and organizations for recommitting. (In more stable structures the weight of tradition discourages innovation, and consciousness of alternatives is low, so that change is doubly difficult.) While this proposition has not been put to the test, it does seem that post-modern societies would benefit more from a rising level of consciousness and suffer more from its lack, because the more options available, the greater the possibility that the reviewing process will ignore some relevant ones.

In sum, societal consciousness may help units to become more the masters of their actions and to realize more of their goals—i.e., to become more active. As consciousness, however, also tends to reduce spontaneity and increase instrumentality, an increase of consciousness without a parallel increase in the other components of the active orientation (knowledge, decision-making, power, and consensus-building capacity) may "dry up" the commitment of the group and weaken rather than strengthen its activeness.

NOTES

*Detailed references will be found in *The Active Society*, pp. 244–248.

1. Warren Breed and Thomas Ktsanes, "Pluralistic Ignorance in the Process of Opinion Formation," *Public Opinion Quarterly*, Vol. 25 (1961), pp. 382–392.

2. Alex Bein, *Theodore Hertzl: A Biography* (Philadelphia: The Jewish Publication Society of America, 1940), p. 116.

3. Saul D. Alinsky, "The War on Poverty—Political Pornography," *Journal of Social Issues*, Vol. 21 (1965), pp. 41–47.

4. Herbert A. Simon, Donald Smithburg, and Victor A. Thompson, *Public Administration* (New York: Knopf, 1959), pp. 130–133.

5. Raymond A. Bauer, Ithiel de Sola Pool, and Lewis Anthony Dexter. *American Business and Public Policy: The Politics of Foreign Trade* (New York: Atherton Press, 1963), pp. 408–413.

6. John Leo, "I.Q.s of Underprivileged Infants Raised Dramatically by Tutors," *New York Times*, December 26, 1968. The article refers to studies of very young children at Catholic and Syracuse Universities.

7. Jacob Katz, *Exclusiveness and Tolerance* (London: Oxford University Press, 1961).

8. Richard Cloward and Frances Fox Piven, "The Birth of a Movement," *Nation*, Vol. 204 (1967), pp. 582–588.

9. Warner Bloomberg Jr. and Florence W. Rosenstock, chap. 11 in Bloomberg and Henry J. Schmandt, *Power, Poverty and Urban Policy* (Beverly Hills: Sage, 1968).

10. Carl Bakal, *The Right to Bear Arms* (New York: McGraw-Hill, 1966).

CHAPTER IX

Two Methods of Decision-Making*

When a group or society faces a problem, how does it respond? We daresay no modern society would follow the extreme traditionalism of a folk society like Bali.[1] There, when a problem arises, the elder chiefs tell how a similar situation was faced in the past, and that becomes the solution. "What was good enough for my father. . . ."

In the preceding five chapters we have examined knowledge as a key cybernetic control element. Now we will see how that knowledge is put into practice—how it is *implemented.* This chapter and the next will consider *decision-making,* and then we move on to the topic of power.

If modern societies do not respond like the Balinese, how do they face problems? *How are vague "goals" translated into specific acts?* We come now to the "steering wheel" of the self-guiding society.

Decision-Making Slighted: The Example of Modernization[2]

Actually, sociologists have not treated the topic of decision-making with the care and devotion it deserves. Instead, when they study the action or change of a group, they tend to explore "background" conditions (e.g., the economic assets of the unit, its power constellation, education levels of the population, or the degree of achievement-orientation of its leaders and people). They apparently feel that these "background" factors explain

Notes for this Chapter are on pages 101 and 102.

change and non-change. For example, they might assume that because a country is poor in material assets and capital, it can develop only slowly. Or that, because of the revolution of rising expectations, democratic elites cannot much limit the availability of consumer goods. Differences in decision-making procedures are considered either "dependent" variables or trivial. Above all, the human dynamics in decision-making have been slighted.

In contrast, the theory of societal guidance suggests that decision-makers have more autonomy, more options. Background factors cannot be ignored, of course, but they are viewed as setting a broad framework for many possible decisions. An effective elite in a poor country, for example, might defer consumption increase despite rising expectations (as the Soviet Union did) and tip the scales in favor of developing heavy industry. We are not saying, of course, which decision is "better"; we are claiming that the decision-making process is crucial to goal attainment, and thus deserves study.

To continue the example of the developing nations, many of these countries are not overpopulated or poor in resources, but *are poor in control capacities.* The quality of their elites, their knowledge, and their decision-making needs to be included in analyzing their success or failure in modernizing. In 1930, for instance, the level of economic development of Canada and Argentina was similar, on several key indicators. Since that time Canada has continued to develop; Argentina remains underdeveloped. A typical background-condition approach would use the Weberian model by stressing the presence of the Protestant element in one country and its absence in the other and correlating this with attitudes toward capitalism. What the theory of societal guidance would add is attention to the responsive-democratic government of Canada as against the authoritarian leadership of Argentina. We gain in understanding by contrasting the development of a given country under different governments using different decision-making procedures (e.g. Peron and Illia in Argentina). Or indeed, in the U.S., the indifferent development under Harding, Coolidge, and Hoover as against more "active" administrations.

Moreover, the quality of decision-making becomes increasingly important the more active a society is. This is why, in the final decades of the 20th century, the study of decision-making assumes new significance. The active orientation seeks to discover the conditions under which *men can set their course of action,* as against being swept along by the vagaries of "natural processes." With knowledge and commitment to goals, men can use reason to make decisions about how best to gain those goals.

The Specification of Societal Commitment

Decision-making specifies goals. Without specification, goals remain vague and abstract hopes. Thus goals and values are *translated* into specific plans—ways and means—for a given course of action. Decision-making is, however, not a one-shot affair. A decision is reached, but it must be implemented and is subject to all the constraints of any action in a complex social system of differentiated parts, pulling and hauling in various directions. In the ensuing process, the initial decision may be either fulfilled or weakened, reinforced or lost, clarified or distorted. Continual specification is required, and this is largely what decision-making entails.

Structurally, decision-making appears at the point of meeting between the cybernetic centers and the implementation processes (both are part of the controlling overlayer). Thus, the *inputs into a decision* (which, in this sense, "precede" implementation) include all of the cybernetic factors, and we restate them here: the *knowledge* of the actor, used to chart alternative routes and to explore their expected consequences; the actor's *consciousness* of himself and of others inside and outside the controlling overlayer; and the actor's general *commitment* to goals and values which are to be specified in the decision-making process. Next, *implementation "follows" the decision process in that decisions are communicated to the sub-units and power is applied to enforce them.* (If we add mobilization of support and consensus-formation, we have here the major variables in the active orientation.)

Decision-making, then, is a synthesizing process within the controlling centers, in which knowledge and commitment are fused and related to considerations of *how goals are to be specified and implemented.* Very importantly, it is also the point at which the element of choice (and thus freedom) is most explicit; decision-making is the most deliberate and voluntaristic domain of social conduct. It most clearly distinguishes *controlled* from *ongoing* processes.

By *decision* we mean a *conscious* choice between two or more alternatives. Not all choices are conscious, but unconscious choices are not decisions. Many social actors are unaware of all the choices available to them. It is the *role of knowledge* to "discover" the options which are present but invisible to the myopic actor. The *range of options* is usually greater than it seems to the passive actor. The number of human groups that fail to realize this runs, literally, into the millions.

While many volumes have been written about decision-making,[3] and some political scientists have developed macroscopic approaches,[4] most are deficient for a theory of societal guidance. They are either merely descriptive of a given decision or are normative "how to" prescriptions,[5] or they deal with persons (voters, consumers) rather than with groups or societies.[6] On the last point consider the difference between a housewife puzzling whether to buy Brand X or Brand Y, and General Motors pondering whether to produce an automobile powered by steam or electricity rather than by the internal combustion engine.

Current writing about decision-making builds on two quite different strategies—the rationalist and the incrementalist theories. We shall examine both for their suitability to the active society and shall suggest a third approach—mixed scanning—which seems superior to both.

TWO METHODS OF DECISION-MAKING

"Rational" Decision-Making

Using *instrumental rationality,*[7] the decision-maker becomes aware of a problem, studies it, carefully weighs alternative means to its solution, and makes a choice. Criteria for the optimal decision are derived from the values of the group. To be "rational," the managers must be free from "particularistic" and "affective" commitments such as obligations to kinsmen, friends, class, or caste. Detachment, neutrality, a highly calculative orientation, and "coolness" underlie the decision. The affective ties of the "warm" personality and all favoritism and irrelevancies are to be avoided. The social structure thought to be most congenial to rational decision-making is the achievement-oriented, entrepreneurial "western" society.

CRITICISMS OF THE RATIONAL MODEL: INTRINSIC

The criticisms of this "rational" model are many and quite convincing. What is "rationality," in the first place? What is relevant and what is irrelevant (e.g., in a nation or in a corporation is the family not relevant—and if so, why is it neglected in the models?). Is a President's loyalty to a trusted colleague not relevant, and might not this loyalty influence an important decision? Various studies demonstrate that "expressive" elements play important parts in all human endeavors. The calculating man is not necessarily the most effective man.

More specifically, criticisms of the rational model have taken these three directions:

1. Success in goal attainment means commitment to the goal, and commitment is an emotional—thus non-rational—state. The greater the rationality and detachment, the more the emotions are suppressed, and the greater the chance that commitment will recede. It was Weber who pointed out that the Protestant Ethic was originally a means to a religious goal (success in work was a sign of salvation), but eventually the religious value atrophied and self-denial remained with no other worldly goal to legitimize it.[8] Some bureaucratic rules

similarly survive long after their ostensible functions have receded beyond memory. Studies of problem-solving groups have shown that *instrumental leadership is often complemented by expressive leadership to maintain commitment,* as seen in the role of the yarn-spinning labor mediator or the nurse who plays the "mother" to the physician's "father" role in patient care.[9] The same may hold at times for other "non-rational" criteria for the selection of means—favoritism, "kickbacks," or the diversion of a highway to memorialize a shrine. Thus rationality should be viewed not as merely instrumental but as a balance between canny means-selection and the maintenance of goal commitment in the team.

2. All groups have several goals and several kinds of needs or "functional problems," so that overspecialization may threaten survival. To seek goals entails the propitiation of all system needs. When coal for the locomotive is scarce, one is tempted to burn planks from the cars—with obvious secondary damage to the system. Poor maintenance of tools reduces present demands on personnel, but may undermine later performance. Likewise, proper attention is needed for such tasks as recruitment, training, morale, and tension management. Some activities servicing the various needs may require constant supervision, as when in both religion and education the tasks of fundraising, enrollment, and building construction threaten to replace more fundamental goals.

3. Since a group is committed to more than one goal at any time, and since not one but many persons and sub-units are in the game, it is very difficult to gain agreement on just what goal or goals are being sought. For example, American leaders for 200 years have enunciated societal goals as freedom, democracy, security, equality, rationality, and progress. Attempts at ranking such a list seem doomed to failure, as there are no agreed-upon criteria to suggest the relative weights of the values. Few decisions pit "good" against "bad"; more often, various shades of "gray" are in dispute. Further, means are limited, and the commitment of resources to one goal denies them as means to a second goal. It is suggested, therefore,

that the narrow notion of instrumental rationality be replaced with the broader "comprehensive rationality," [10] so that elites gain control not only of the relationships between the means but also *the relationships between goals and their respective means.* Thus the military, responsible for national security, may seek to economize in its choice of weapons. Yet a balanced budget is not one of the military's goals—therefore, a more comprehensive review of military decisions must be maintained at a higher level, i.e., by "civilian" spokesmen.

INABILITY TO MEET THE REQUIREMENTS

Thus far, we have outlined three criticisms of rationality as a guide to societal decision-making which are intrinsic to the concept. This is not all. We turn now to an extrinsic criticism—that the model is not applicable *because decision-makers neither can nor do meet its requirements.* Since instrumental rationality is inadequate even intrinsically, we focus on the shortcomings of comprehensive rationality.

Experts agree on the four main requirements for rational decision-making: [11] (1) information about alternative courses of action and their costs and consequences; (2) calculation of the alternative outcomes in terms of their meaning for the various values and for various combinations of means; (3) a set of agreed-upon values on the basis of which to select goals and to judge the consequences of alternative plans; and (4) an exhaustive survey of all relevant variables and alternatives, since an unstudied item may be the optimal one. We have already argued that the third requirement cannot be met.

Although, as we said earlier, information is becoming much more available in post-modern society through the spread of education, R&D, and new communications media, *decision-makers never have all the information they need.* They will certainly have some information and will be getting more from their knowledge elites, but "some" is never "enough." Staff meetings are forever plagued with the admission by experts that "we just don't know the answer to that question." And by the time one problem is solved, others spring up in tantalizing fashion. True, computers help in the collection of information and in its processing from a "raw" state, but in addition much old-fashioned "digging" for data and much complex analysis of the data are required.

In most discussions of the actual capacities of decision-makers, it is assumed that decisions are made by individuals—the atomistic fallacy.[12] It is of course true that some boards are dominated by "strong" men. We hold that more often decisions are made by societal units—e.g., by Congress or an executive committee, with differentiated roles at play. If the several executives were isolated from each other, they would arrive at different decisions than they reached in concert. Decision-makers affect each other. Studies reveal that opinions given in private undergo modification when others are privy to the exchange.[13] "Ego influences alter" under the press of social interaction, past, present, and future. Decision-making is a collective experience *sans par,* whether in cabinet, board, or committee, and rationality bows to position, prestige, interpersonal influence, and the hedonistic calculus.

As was suggested, the executives may not even know what information is necessary, what questions are to be asked, what variables are to be plugged into the computer. This ignorance may be a minor matter with such problems as predicting the traffic flow across the George Washington Bridge, but the issues we are considering are more complex. When men of differing status and ideology are interacting with one another and the goals and interests of competing organizations are up for grabs, the computer program represents only the visible portion of the iceberg. If this is true for conventional situations, the uncertainty is compounded in changing, emergent situations—the kind typically encountered in post-modern society.[14]

We have argued that the evolution of recent structural shifts in knowledge production and analysis allows political elites to delegate some areas of decision-making to experts. This occasional retreat of political elites has increased the realm of technical competence, to a degree diminishing the scope of normative and political conflict. But this shift to knowledge as the basis of judgments occurs mainly at the earlier (or lower) levels of policy; the "higher" levels will probably continue to be determined by normative and political (thus not necessarily rational) considerations.

Incrementalism: "Muddling Through"

Several critics of the rational model suggest a second approach to decision-making—*incrementalism.* This method, they claim, avoids the overwhelming difficulties of the rational model and is also descriptive of the way decisions are actually made in pluralist societies. It advocates a "piecemeal" strategy which some call "muddling through." Simon has noted that most decision-makers do not even try to optimize, but settle for *satisficing* decisions, *relatively* satisfactory approximations of their values. Only if the goal-search is badly frustrated is a quest launched for an alternative.

The fullest presentation of this position is given by Charles E. Lindblom.[15] In this scheme, executives do not attempt a comprehensive survey and evaluation. *Rather than adjusting means to goals,* "ends are chosen that are appropriate to available or nearly available means"; means justify ends. There is no one decision; problems are not "solved." There is rather a "never-ending series of attacks" on the issues through successive analyses and policy-making. The incremental approach is deliberately exploratory. One route is tried, and the unforeseen consequences are left to be discovered and treated by subsequent increments. Even the criteria by which increments are evaluated are developed and adapted in the course of action.

This approach assumes that in typical pluralist societies power is distributed among a variety of groupings, parties, and factions in the legislature. There is no single center of power but rather a continual "give-and-take" among the competing units.[16] Thus in the U.S. the President must secure the support of the country and its interest groups and agencies, and must adjust to their demands as they adjust to his. Each unit has a kind of "veto-power" over the proposals of the others. There are no intrinsically good or bad commodities or ideas, just those worked out in coalition and compromise. Thus while incrementalism rejects many of the assumptions of the rational model, both share a key conceptual theme of utilitarianism: atomism.

CRITIQUE OF INCREMENTALISM

Our criticism of incrementalism recognizes that it is the only existing alternative to rationalist decision-making, and that it does describe how pluralistic modern societies, especially the U.S., make their decisions. *Two major weaknesses,* however, mar its usefulness. First, this kind of atomistic competition reflects, in the end, the interests of the *most powerful groupings* in society. Decisions over-represent the strong and penalize the weak. The poor, the ethnic minorities, "consumers," even urban people in a society whose Congress is dominated by rural and suburban interests—these large segments lack power and therefore a place at the decision-making table. Societal responsiveness, thus, will be shortchanged. (In fairness to the incrementalists, it should be noted that they discern factors which soften this rather harsh picture: Some weak minority groups which become intensively committed will in fact be heard,[17] and common values accepted by the elites will bring a measure of altruism to the decision.) Second, incrementalism also ignores *overdue innovations.* Individuals and units tend to become adjusted to the situation, like plants, robots, or members of a utopian blueprint. A "bit" perspective holds sway and the society drifts, thus inviting eventual angry challenges from those who decide to work for a realization of cherished societal goals. Until this moment of confrontation, as one critic of incrementalism has said, we "stagger through history like a drunk putting one disjointed incremental foot after another." [18]

Both of these weaknesses in incrementalism are pointed up

in a review of disaster studies.[19] In the hours following a disaster (e.g., a tornado in a city), the established authority structure is weakened, and new HQs form which allocate resources on a new basis—the basis of need and urgency. It can be argued that this is a very "rational" way of handling the emergency. Decisions are made and carried out on the grounds of what must be done, without regard to past privilege or tradition. The normal constraints of contract and property are undercut by a new system of priorities. Gradually, of course, the old equilibrium is re-established, and decisions are made on the older, possibly less "rational" basis.

NOTES

*Detailed references will be found in *The Active Society,* pp. 273–281.

1. Margaret Mead, "Public Opinion Mechanisms among Primitive Peoples," *Public Opinion Quarterly,* Vol. 1 (1937), pp. 5–16.

2. This section draws from Amitai Etzioni, "Toward a Theory of Societal Guidance," *American Journal of Sociology,* Vol. 73 (September, 1967), pp. 173–187.

3. Martin Shubik, "Studies and Theories of Decision-Making," *Administrative Science Quarterly,* Vol. 3 (1958), pp. 289–306.

4. Richard C. Snyder and Glenn D. Paige, "The United States Decision to Resist Aggression in Korea," *ibid.,* Vol. 3 (1958), pp. 341–379; Allen S. Whiting, *China Crosses the Yalu* (New York: Macmillan, 1960); and Martin Patchen, "Decision Theory in the Study of National Action," *Journal of Conflict Resolution,* Vol. 9 (1965), pp. 164–176.

5. Raymond A. Bauer, "Problem Solving in Organizations: A Functional Point of View," in Merwin M. Hargrove, Ike H. Harrison, and Eugene L. Swearingen (eds.), *Business Policy Cases* (Homewood, Ill.: Richard D. Irwin, 1963), pp. 29–32.

6. Paul Wasserman and Fred S. Silander, *Decision-Making: An Annotated Bibliography* (Ithaca, New York: Cayuga Press, 1958).

7. For an example, see Roger W. Jones, "The Model as a Decision-Maker's Dilemma," *Public Administration Review,* Vol. 24 (1964), pp. 158–160.

8. Max Weber, *The Protestant Ethic and the Spirit of Capitalism,* trans. by Talcott Parsons (New York: Scribner, 1964), pp. 180–182.

9. Talcott Parsons, *The Social System, op. cit.,* pp. 79–88, 127, 334, 385, 401–403, 409–410.

10. Our concept of comprehensive rationality is close to Mannheim's "substantive rationality." Karl Mannheim, *Man and Society in an Age of Reconstruction* (New York: Harcourt, Brace, 1940).

11. Jan Tinbergen, *Economic Policy, Principles and Design* (Amsterdam: North Holland, 1956), pp. 11 ff.

12. William J. Gore and J. W. Dyson (eds.), *The Making of Decisions* (New York: Free Press, 1964), p. 1.

13. Raymond L. Gorden, "Interaction Between Attitude and the Definition of the Situation in the Expression of Opinion," *American Sociological Review*, Vol. 17 (Feb., 1952), pp. 50–58.

14. Robert Boguslaw, *The New Utopians* (Englewood Cliffs: Prentice-Hall, 1964), chap 1.

15. Charles E. Lindblom, "The Science of 'Muddling Through,'" *Public Administration Review*, Vol. 19 (1959), pp. 79–99.

16. Aaron Wildavsky and Arthur Hammond, "Comprehensive versus Incremental Budgeting in the Department of Agriculture," *Administrative Science Quarterly*, Vol. 10 (1965), pp. 321–346, esp. p. 323.

17. Robert A. Dahl, *A Preface to Democratic Theory* (Chicago: University of Chicago Press, 1956), pp. 103 ff.

18. Kenneth Boulding in a review of *Strategy of Decision, American Sociological Review*, Vol. 29 (1964), p. 931.

19. E. L. Quarantelli and Russell Dynes, "Operational Problems of Organizations in Disasters," in *1967 Emergency Operations Symposium* (Santa Monica: System Development Corporation, 1967), pp. 151–175.

CHAPTER X

Mixed Scanning as More Active Decision-Making*

What we need is a method of decision-making which promises more activation than the two types we have described and rejected. The model we recommend is called *mixed scanning.*

Specifically, we want a strategy that is less exacting than the rationalistic one but not so constricting as incrementalism, not so utopian as rationalism but not so conservative as incrementalism, one that can be used but not one that legitimates myopic, elite-oriented, non-innovating policies. In concrete terms, we believe that an empirical study would show that *many executives today use mixed scanning, and find it effective.*

An example of mixed scanning: Weather satellites hold two cameras. One takes broad-angle pictures covering large segments of the sky like a U.S. national road map. The other lens photographs much smaller segments but in much greater detail. Rather than flooding and confusing the analyst with great detail, the dual scanning device gets undetailed but encompassing pictures of the sky *and then scans for signs of trouble* (e.g., possible hurricane clouds). The second camera *explores these danger points in detail.* This procedure also holds for such photo planes as the U-2 and reconnaissance satellites. The investment (financial and otherwise) is less than with "rational" strategies. Continual alertness, of course, is required to make up for the savings. Thus the 1962 scanning of Cuba was sharply increased after too little reconnaissance left the U.S. unaware of the positioning of Soviet missiles until they were almost fully erected.[1]

Notes for this Chapter are on pages 111 and 112.

Similar procedures are often employed in social research. A general problem-area may tantalize one sociologist. He discusses it with colleagues and students. In his reading, he goes to books in that field and monitors his "broad angle" reading for clues relevant to the new problem. Eventually he "defines the issue" by stating one or more hypotheses. At this point "exploratory" interviews may be conducted; respondents are asked very broad questions (e.g., "How do you feel about race relations in the U.S. today?"). Answers are followed up in depth, so that *great detail* (the second camera) from a wide range of sources is fed into the project. Meanwhile staff is being formed, funds raised, equipment assembled, and so on. A questionnaire is prepared, pretested, and administered so that specific answers can complement the broad interview. Further exploratory interviews may be made to clarify points left uncertain from the tabulated frequencies, and further reading done to chart earlier related contributions. Thus various "cameras" (with idiographic and nomothetic "lenses") are kept at work as research decisions are being made.

Scanning need not be restricted to two levels; there can be more, as the planners' awareness of needs changes over time. *Scanning (and almost all decision-making) combines the collecting, processing, and evaluation of information with the process of making choices.* As the actor "scans," he "takes in" information and simultaneously explores possible alternative actions. While these two tasks can be separated for analytical purposes, they go hand in hand, and we shall treat them jointly.

In general, each of the two elements in mixed scanning helps to reduce the effects of the particular shortcomings of the other. Incrementalism reduces the unrealistic aspects of rationalism by limiting the details required in fundamental decisions, and contextuating rationalism helps to overcome the conservative slant of incrementalism by exploring longer-run alternatives. The annual Congressional debate over the budget, the President's State of the Union message, and meetings of the Council of Economic Advisers have some elements of such a strategy in

U.S. decision-making. We argue that these elements make for a third approach which is at once more realistic and more effective than the other two.

Bit Decisions and Fundamental Decisions

The incrementalists do not deny the existence of *fundamental decisions* such as a declaration of war. They do argue, however, that incremental decisions are much more common. We agree, but add that (1) most incremental decisions anticipate or specify fundamental decisions and (2) the cumulative value of the incremental decisions is greatly affected by the underlying fundamental decisions. *It is a fundamental decision, not "bit" decisions, which "turns a corner" in the policy of a group or society.*

Thus it is not enough and not complete to show, as Richard Fenno did, that Congress makes primarily bit changes in the national budget (a comparison of one year's budget for a federal agency with that of the preceding year showed only a 10 per cent or lower difference, on many occasions).[2] Nor is it enough to show that the defense budget does not change much in terms of its percentage of the national budget or that the budget remains much the same in terms of its percentage of the GNP. *These bit changes are often indicative of trends launched at critical turning points at which fundamental decisions were made.* The defense budget increased at the start of the Korean war in 1950 from 5.0 per cent of the GNP to 10.3 per cent in 1951. The fact that it stayed at this level (between 9.0 and 10.3 per cent of the GNP) did reflect minor incremental decisions, but these were made *within the basic decision to enter the war.* Fenno's own figures, moreover, show almost as many changes of above 20 per cent as below this level. Several budget changes zoomed 100 per cent or more, and 24 rose by 50 per cent or more.

Once Congress decided to establish a national space agency, it voted small incremental changes for several years. But again, a decisive, fundamental decision had been made. Large decisions of this type place liens, however incremental, on future years. What may appear to be a series of bit decisions is, in effect, the extension of one fundamental decision.

Evaluating Decisions

We assume that decision-making strategies *can be evaluated* as to their relative effectiveness. Incrementalists deny this; they hold that values cannot be scaled and summarized. We believe, on the other hand, that some ranking and evaluation is possible, so that elites can "keep up" on their quality of performance and implement programs with maximal effect.

Many projects have one primary goal. For example: economically desalting sea water, increasing birth control, reducing price inflation by one-half over a two-year period. Other goals may also be advanced in the process but are secondary (for example, increasing the country's R&D sector by investment in desalting). Thus an evaluation is quite possible with regard to the success or failure of the primary goal, and secondary consequences can be noted as well. We can arbitrarily weigh the primary goal as several times more important than the secondary ones. When there are several primary goals (e.g., teaching, therapy, and research in a university hospital), we can still compare projects—project X may be "good" for research, "poor" for teaching, and so on.

An informal scaling of values is not so difficult as the incrementalists imagine. In the State Department, for example, costs of given activities are multiplied by a number representing the rank of their objectives.[3] In one case, the exchange of Fulbright professors may contribute to "cultural prestige and mutual respect," "educational development," and "gaining entree." These might be given scale numbers such as 8, 6, and 5, respectively. These numbers are then multiplied by the costs of the program, and the resulting figure is in turn multiplied with an ingenious figure representing the "importance" to the U.S. of the countries with which we have cultural relations. When the resulting figures are revised on the basis of judgment and experience (as in mixed scanning), a certain tiny Middle-Eastern country may turn out to be more "important" (on the goals in question) than a large European one.

This, to be sure, is primitive evaluation, but since full detailed rationalism may well be impossible, such truncated reviews seem more effective than "muddling through," by providing some basis for active decision-making.[4]

Social Factors in Decision-Making

When an elite engages in the decision-making process, more than intellectual procedures are at work. Decision-making is as *socio-political* as any other distributive process involving hope of gain and risk of loss. As always, *social relationships* are at play between individuals occupying roles in groups (political elites, knowledge elites, experts, the implied presence of active publics, voters, stockholders, and the like). Conflict between actors and sub-units is frequent. Pressure is being applied at many points. Discussion of these social factors affecting the decision-making strategy follows.

LEAD TIME AND SLACK

All decisions are made within a very real context. Part of the context involves a time-sequence component; earlier decisions may create the conditions for later ones. Thus at each decision-making round, the elites have some *options* they can exploit but also some *conditions*, set by earlier decisions, which are fixed and cannot be changed. The longer the series of decisions being related, the longer the "lead time," the more important is the *anticipatory capacity* of the elite for its active orientation. With more lead time, there is greater need for the elite to scan in depth and to anticipate the consequences of potential decisions. In national monetary policy, for example, "Keynesian" approaches which anticipate fluctuations in the business cycle provide governments with the capacity—at least, until recent years—to head off crippling depressions or inflations. The result has been greater efficiency in the economy.

When options are related in time but decisions are made incrementally, crisis-management is likely to result. When the inadequacy of policy becomes obvious, large investments ("crash programs") may be launched to reduce the problem, and this accentuates the strain on other parts of the system.

One way of hedging against such crisis is to maintain "slack" in the system. Corporations, like armies, reserve some assets and energies not committed to any specific use. When scanning shows the need for action in a certain sector, these assets can be quickly recommitted; costlier crash programs become unnecessary.

THE ELITE'S SELF-INTEREST IN SCANNING

The quality of decision-making performance has, of course, consequences *for the elite itself.* Most elites, naturally enough, wish to keep power. A double standard pervades their decision-making: their wish to advance both the interests of their group and *their own interests* as well. It is not that most elites deliberately violate basic social values to stay in office (although history knows such cases). The values sacrificed for "political" considerations are often peripheral, such as loyalty to friends, candor, and fiscal integrity. Elites often argue that they must disregard some values to advance the rest. This "conflict of interest" question and the possibility of corruption it involves has consequences for decision-making.

In stable societies, the double-standard perspective usually favors an incremental strategy, since it permits the elites to avoid fundamental changes which are often politically dangerous. Thus elites keep power, and societal needs are *apparently* being served as well.

MIXED SCANNING AS MORE ACTIVE DECISION-MAKING

Mixed scanning, however, is a more effective strategy even for a bifocal elite, because when incremental decisions are made in situations in which fundamental decisions are called for, *the elite suffers as well as the unit.* In such cases the elites may be removed from office. President Truman, for example, treated the cessation of the Korean war in a typically incremental fashion; General Eisenhower promised to terminate it at once, which was one reason for his defeat of Adlai Stevenson. Truman's incrementalism paid few dividends for himself and his advisers. Eight years later, President Eisenhower was charged with incrementing on the domestic front; Senator Kennedy promised to get the country "moving again." In these two instances entire administrations were replaced, and the society initiated a basic change.

Effective decision-makers would seem to need a "rule" of strategy: *When criticism shows that a policy is ineffective, stop incrementing and turn to more encompassing scanning.*

While we believe that most actors will do better by using mixed scanning in most situations, there are exceptions. In general, the less malleable the environment or the actor and the fewer available resources, the less damage incrementalism will cause. The more malleable the situation and the actor and the more resources available, the less helpful is incrementalism and the more encompassing scanning is called for in the decision-making mix. The rationalistic approach seems inappropriate in both circumstances.

POWER AND VALUES

Power and *normative commitment* are two important factors, along with knowledge, that enter the decision-making process. Thus the industrial management of a corporation—presumably more "rational" and less "political" than most elites—decides on the relative weight of dividends, reinvestments, and wage increases not only on "economic" grounds, but on such "power" considerations as these: How many of the managers are also stockholders, how well organized the workers are, the pressure of governmental tax agencies on firms that do not reinvest, and so on. The power held by elites varies. Some elites are little more than "brokers" who *reflect* the relative power of member-units. Others have more power than all member-units combined (but the latter can never be completely ignored). Many elites fall in between these two extremes, but all recognize the fact of power, and its constraints in decision-making.

Elites often express normative commitments when decisions are being made, and these too may influence policy. Some values adhere closely to the overall *perspective* of the unit; others come close to being "unthinkable." A unit which favors a plan that is considered questionable in normative or knowledge terms will be forced to apply much more of its power to gain a decision.

The relationship between values, knowledge, and power is illustrated in the presidential campaign of Senator Eugene McCarthy. When he announced his candidacy in late 1967 he was relatively weak on all three components. When he gained the backing of many youth and anti-war groups, and when the Tet offensive in Vietnam early in 1968 showed that the war was far from being "won," his candidacy became more tenable and still other factions decided to support him. The gain was not great enough, of course, to win nomination at the Democratic convention.

In no case can power be ignored among the forces that contribute to decision-making. Knowledge-producing units can exert their influence to a certain extent: by showing that a rival group's information is incorrect, by the skill with which they present their case, or by forming coalitions with other decision-making parties. A government, however, may ignore information (say, about an imminent coup), but not the tanks crashing the gates of the Presidential palace. A President might ignore the information that Congress will defeat a bill that he favors, but this will not alter the fact that when the vote comes, the bill will fail; the decision will be shaped directly by power.

Implementating Decisions and Activation

If power is a component in decision-making, it is the key factor in *implementation.* The power involved in both is often virtually the same force; decision-making and implementation are closely interwoven acts. Early decisions shape the power which affects later decisions, and the more the initial decision took the relevant power into account, the more effective implementation will be. In early decisions the actor is in effect testing his power to gain his course *before* announcing his preferred plan!

Thus control is not just a process of information-collection and analysis and the expression of commitments, but also a process of the mobilization and use of assets. Other things being equal, the more assets, the more effective the decisions—thus the relevance of power-analysis for an adequate theory of decision-making.

In summarizing our discussion of decision-making, it seems clear that both the rationalistic and the incremental models promote inactivity in the unit and frustration in the elites. Mixed scanning, on the other hand, seems to permit the greater realization of goals; it can "work." The combination of bit-incrementation with contextual decision-making provides both a short-run probing and a long-run criterion for evaluation, both a realization of the inability to consider all alternatives and a trigger mechanism to recall broader considerations when necessary. Above all, it allows for setting informed and committed vision on the road to attempts to transform the societal unit—that is, it promotes activism.

Having sketched the role of power in decision-making, we now turn directly to the analysis of power as an implementing force in the guiding of societal action.

NOTES

*Detailed references will be found in *The Active Society,* pp. 305–309.

CYBERNETIC FACTORS

1. Elie Abel, *The Missile Crisis* (Philadelphia: Lippincott, 1966), pp. 17–32, esp. p. 26.

2. Richard F. Fenno, Jr., *The Power of the Purse* (Boston: Little Brown, 1966), pp. 266 ff.

3. Virginia Held, "PPBS Comes to Washington," *The Public Interest*, No. 4 (Summer 1966), pp. 102–115.

4. For a guide to problems of program evaluation, see Edward A. Suchman, *Evaluative Research* (New York: Russell Sage Foundation, 1967).

PART III

IMPLEMENTING FACTORS

CHAPTER XI

Power: Its Strength and Limitations*

Power is exerted in almost all social relations and will certainly loom large in the self-guiding society. This is because *the realization of most societal goals requires the use of power.* All societies and large groupings have a distributive function: They possess assets and rewards which are distributed among the various sub-groups. "Who gets what" reflects the power system. In this chapter we examine the strengths and limitations of power (as an implementing mechanism) and its relation to communication (a cybernetic mechanism).

We define power as the capacity to overcome part or all of the resistance offered by other units. The most powerful units can overcome most of the resistance of all the others. We speak, of course, not of an individual person or small group; we are focusing on macrosocial relations.

A main objection to the use of the concept of power is that power can be assessed only *after* X has overcome the resistance of Y. To avoid this difficulty, we will consider power as a generalized capacity, rather than action in a single encounter. Thus on the basis of past observation, we can make fairly accurate estimates of the power of X and Y, and so on.

Power as the Commitment of Assets

Assets are possessions of a unit which may be converted into power, or may not; they are a potential. Power, on the

Notes for this Chapter are on page 127.

other hand, is the energy actually employed, from the unit's assets, in a given engagement.

This distinction between assets and power, and the notion of the generalized power of a group, is useful for three reasons. First, it explains submission even when there is no actual exercise of power. A group of discontented workers will decide not to challenge the employer when they recognize his assets, which at the moment include the passivity of a majority of their fellow workers; also, when the sensed probability of being treated punitively is higher than the group is willing to accept.

Second, a group powerful in one sector may be relatively weak in another. Yet there remains a generalized "halo" effect. For example, the U.S. has enormous power in many sectors, but in voting in the General Assembly of the U.N. its vote counts for no more than that of a tiny country. Actually, however, the economic power of the U.S. in Latin America gives it considerable influence over the votes of these countries in the General Assembly—and the same influence prevails in the Organization of American States. Thus generalized power casts a relatively long shadow across several sectors.

Third, a group may decide to "lay out" of a campaign, committing no assets. In such a case, *a group with fewer assets committed to the issue* will show the most power and attain victory. Thus many Democratic party leaders committed less of their assets to the Humphrey campaign in 1968, while Republicans—the minority party—invested more heavily in Nixon. Of course, such a victory may promote greater mobilization of the losing side in future contests, so there is the added factor of "winning the battle but losing the war." Atomistic power analysis, focusing on each single instance, would be unable to encompass the long-run series; collectivistic power analysis, focusing on differences in gross assets, may expect the affluent actor to prevail in the first—and all succeeding—encounters. "Giants" simply do not "win them all"—from Napoleon to the U.S. military-industrial complex to the U.S. armed forces (e.g., Korea, Vietnam).

Every social unit constantly chooses (not always consciously) what to do with its assets. Assets can be *consumed* (used to satisfy immediate needs), *preserved* for later use, *invested* to increase the asset base, or *converted* into societal power. Thus assets are stable or structural; power is more dynamic or processual. Elites, using their best knowledge, make these decisions. When control is effective, a small gain in assets will produce marked increments in power. Added resources will afford little gain to a fumbling affluent unit, while a relatively small gain in its guidance mechanisms will strengthen action capacity. For a pressure group, the opening of a Washington office and the hiring of a writer is a small investment but a marked step-up in the group's potential influence.

Greater Power by Improving Control: Conversion

While both factors are operative, it seems that in the short run, the *capacity to improve control* is higher than the capacity to increase assets. In crisis situations, for instance, "hidden" powers may pop up; that is, the group overcomes resistance (of varied forms) which previously was thought to be invincible, and the giant is slain. This emerges not because new assets are gained, but because the control of assets is shifted and mobilized from relatively private to societal use and from *consumption* to *conversion* into societal power.

In studying and comparing units from this viewpoint, differences in *conversion ratios* and *conversion patterns* are examined. The conversion *ratio* specifies the proportion of the assets used to generate power as compared to the total assets. Within a very few years in the early 1960s, Negroes converted many assets into political power. The conversion *pattern* describes the manner in which assets are assigned to the various areas—narrow or broad in scope, allotted to internal or external usage, and so on.

RECENT TRENDS IN CONVERSION

What are the historical patterns with regard to these ratios and patterns? At first glance it seems that an increasingly higher ratio of assets is devoted to societal uses. But detailed statistical analysis is needed to supply the answer to such questions as whether expenditures for "the public sector" have indeed risen in recent decades.

As to the *conversion pattern*, discussions of the welfare state or welfare capitalism would suggest a historical trend toward an increasingly internally-focused pattern. But the semi-war state of the post-modern world indicates that defense expenditures have risen even more than domestic ones.

Country	GNP	Defense	Per cent	Education	Per cent	Health	Per cent
United States	628,700	51,323	8.2	30,400	4.8	10,000	1.6
Denmark	8,940	255	2.9	300	3.4	190	2.1
Norway	6,200	220	3.5	325	5.2	100	1.6
Sweden	17,200	826	4.8	800	4.7	400	2.3

Figures are in millions of United States dollars equivalents for 1964. See William M. Sprecher, *World-Wide Defense Expenditures and Selected Economic Data, 1964* (Washington, D.C.: United States Arms Control and Disarmament Agency, 1966), pp. 7–8.

The only clear trend in accord with common-sense expectations is in the breadth of societal control: More sectors of societal activity are guided collectively in the post-modern than in the modern period, though the main pattern was established in the last modern century (1845–1945).

One conclusion seems clear: Building an active society will require the conversion of a greater amount *and* ratio of societal assets *to societal use,* since the realization of collective goals seems to lag behind the realization of those more "private" goals served directly by sub-units or by their unguided interaction. Also, more effort will be needed for internal than for external areas. More active societies generally also follow a more internally-oriented pattern.

The scope of guidance will vary by areas. Already the societal guidance of *technology* has begun. The guidance of other areas—the reallocation of wealth and a greater equalization of status-relations—has started, but is not yet sufficiently "energized," as judged by the goals of post-modern societies. The guidance mechanisms, especially as to decision-making, and likewise the function of *fundamental criticism* are the most neglected.

These two dimensions of conversion—ratio and pattern—used in combination characterize a major aspect of the structure of society. Each is an independent variable. Their study, along with the societal asset structure and the system of values—and the relationships among all of these—is put forward as a frame of reference to advance the understanding of societal guidance.

Limitations on Great Power Centers

Sometimes writers (such as Marx and C. Wright Mills) sound as if they accept one giant grouping as all-powerful. For example, "the military-industrial complex" of the U.S. No doubt there is some truth in this belief, but we feel it is just as important to look for *limitations* on this formidable-appearing power.

The power of today may be different tomorrow. In a rapidly changing society, circumstances change many things, including power. A major grouping may decide not to commit its assets to a struggle. Another previously quiet group may rapidly mobilize and capture widespread public support, especially if events are favorable, thus changing the existing consensus. No group commits the same amount of assets to each campaign, year after year. A charismatic leader may enthrall hitherto passive millions. New research reports and fundamental criticism may disclose new problems, as did the Harrington book on poverty in the U.S. and Steinbeck's *The Grapes of Wrath,* dealing with "factories in the fields." A book may dramatize an old problem, as did *Uncle Tom's Cabin* (1852), which mobilized antagonism to slavery.

Equally possible, a powerful group may blunder by actions which violate basic mores and boomerang. Marie Antoinette infuriated the people with her cavalier pronouncement about bread; the brilliant Alcibiades was banished for sacrilegious indiscretions against revered Athenian icons;[1] the Ku Klux Klan might have maintained the tacit approval of responsible southern leaders were it not for murder, wanton brutality, and misuse of members' dues. The powerful American Medical Association was barred from hearings in the House of Representatives for its die-hard opposition to Medicare, which Chairman Mills said was of little help in writing legislation.[2]

Powerful groups, of course, hold great advantages. Deploying their assets wisely, they can deflect or postpone most of the demands of militant groups. While the protest group must exert massive efforts to gain press sympathy and third-party support, its own members may fall away when its leaders are forced to issue temporizing public statements and to bargain with elites.[3] Even if the movement wins public sympathy, public officials can decimate gains by many well-known tactics: tokenism, the granting of symbolic rather than tangible satisfactions, giving the appearance but not the reality of action, the study committee, etc. Thus the Harlem rent strikes of 1964–65, under Jesse Gray, aroused great public interest but won only modest improvements.[4] Perhaps the major consequence of many protests is the fact of mobilization of previously apathetic persons and the formation of more potent organizations.

Further, most groups have *poor knowledge* about their own power as against that of other groups. They will boast great strength, while privately admitting fears of weakness. The sources of power are many and varied and include such intangibles as the effectiveness of a group's elites and lieutenants and its capacity to mobilize loyalty. Some groups with real power actually try to conceal it, in the belief that advertising strength may invite a contest—much like the muscle-man at the beach who is continually being challenged. In fact, if the relative power of various units were completely measurable and if there were a supreme judge to announce the power rankings, little conflict would occur; a basic latent function of conflict, it seems, is to substitute for the absence of clear rankings. Everyone agrees that Team A won the World Series, but in the Socio-Political League the rankings are seldom so clear.

Thus we may say that power is a universal feature of social life but is not omnipotent. Another limitation to absolute power is the values to which people and groups are committed; power is sometimes suspended because people *believe* they should withhold power in this situation—like the storybook hero sparing the life of his defeated antagonist or the Detroit pitcher who, with his team well ahead, threw the ailing Mickey Mantle a "home-run ball" so the latter could gain a notch in the all-time home-run derby. The narrow range of the power of American Presidents and the limitations on the power even of totalitarian leaders and parties are well documented. Power can be exercised only to the extent that power potentials are unevenly distributed among people and groups and that power used is seen as legitimate (e.g., the fate of alcohol Prohibition).

"Communications" Theories and Their Weaknesses

We have argued that power is not omnipotent, but we are far from willing to go to the other extreme. Such a virtual abandonment is epitomized in "communications" theories. For example, Karl W. Deutsch: "Essentially, control involves the transmission of messages, and the understanding of control processes is a branch of communications engineering, not of power engineering."[5] Government is, accordingly, viewed as a communications network, a web of nerves. Once government signals reach the appropriate receiver and are clearly understood, they are expected to produce the appropriate action—not by their power but by the change they produce in the receiver's pattern of information. This theory uses the example of a gun: The force of the shot need not be proportionate to the amount of pressure taken to squeeze the trigger.

In contrast, power analysis assumes that power frequently must be expended (to reduce resistance of various sorts) and that the degree of action is greatly affected by the degree of power mobilized. The gun analogy is cogent: The power of the trigger is minute, quite true, but the thrust of the bullet comes from the power *previously stored* in the gun-powder, which the trigger finally releases. If a government orders its troops to attack, communications analysis can trace the message and its cycle. But the field commander's action is not determined wholly by the signal. He also considers his assets and the larger context: the number and firepower of his troops and the force of the enemy, troop loyalty and morale, and, not least, his picture of the reprisals—government power—that face non-complying officers.

Most people, in fact—parents, teachers, friends, sergeants, employers, supervisors—have had the experience of issuing very clear orders and having them spurned until threats (spanking, firing, punishing) implemented the order. Again, road signs posting speed limits are clear enough, but the Highway Patrol is a much stronger force in implementing safe auto speeds. Hitler's orders were followed more speedily in 1940 than in 1944.

Of course communication is "the" basic social process and does affect action, and the various factors determining the flow or impedence of communication are crucial in the study of social dynamics. It is also a valuable insight that the amount of energy used in transmitting communication is low in proportion to its results (although the investment in building the network has cost heavily). But such communication analysis must be combined with power analysis and *cannot replace it.* We need to document both types of input.

This holds for all kinds of organizations, not just the military. For instance, when the aluminum and copper industries failed to respond in 1965 to President Johnson's signals to refrain from raising their prices, he used his "big artillery," ordering the selling of those metals from government stockpiles—a conversion of assets. Similarly in 1968 he ordered government purchases of steel from those companies which had not raised prices. Signals must be backed by perceived power.

Communication and Power Used Jointly

Political elites must make *two kinds of decisions:* what signals to issue and what power to commit to support them. As we suggest, the asset-power base is much less elastic than the symbols which are the main base of communication. Elites can transmit signals on power "credit," hoping they will have no need to cash it in, or "bluff"—communicate as if they had power when they do not. Of course, to the degree that authentic consensus has been established, communication will suffice, but this is only sometimes the case. It is seldom the case in the competitive "who gets what" society.

To some degree, power and communication can be *substituted* for each other. To use a military illustration, if the goal is to rout an enemy from a jungle, extensive bombing will be fruitless if air intelligence cannot communicate to the aircrews the position of the enemy under the foliage. The more knowledge communicated, the fewer the bombs required; the less that is known and communicated, the greater the bomb-loads for the same results.

Above all, increasing *both* control elements—communication and power—presents the group with more action potential. To illustrate: In a midwestern city, civil rights groups countered urban renewal drives (which destroyed slums before adequate alternative housing was provided) by lying down in front of the bulldozers. This meant civil disobedience, a "costly" operation. Over the years, these groups organized an "early warning" system to discover in advance the target sites for bulldozing. This allowed the groups to mobilize public support by protests to the press and the legislature and to demonstrate, and still—if necessary—to block the bulldozers.

Another approach of significance to societal guidance—the human relations school—almost completely ignored power analysis.[6] Emphasis was placed on leadership style—focusing on understanding and sensitivity to workers' needs, such as affection. If management catered to these needs (as in the famous Hawthorne studies), chances of power struggle, unionization, and increased salary demands would decline. Critics of this school saw a degree of power struggle, conflict, and tension between workers and management as inevitable, and perhaps beneficial in terms of basic human needs.[7]

Actually, it appears that when workers belong to unions which effectively express their sentiments and interests and when they are well paid, communication between management and workers plays a relatively important role; when this is not the case, the effect of communications differences is small. Thus again, power and communication analyses complement rather than negate each other; neither one is either determinative or superfluous.

Communications Skills and Credibility

Once the fact that communication is only one part of control is accepted, the question turns to the ways in which communication and power are related. A main factor here is the communication capacities and skills of the units, because the uses to which assets may be put (their power potential) are difficult to assess. Thus there is a permanent gap between the symbolic and the objective facets of power; this permits the magnification of power *by skillful signals.*

Actors manipulate their power potential and their messages much as poker players do. The effective player gains more from the same hand than a poor player would. Gestures and tactics can win games. Yet gestures must not be too far divorced from the objective base: He who regularly bluffs with poor cards will eventually lose his shirt. Thus some degree of *credibility* in the relations between communication and power is mandatory lest gestures become powerless.

The macroscopic parallels of poker gestures are *threats and promises*.[8] The question becomes the degree of resemblance between fact and gesture. One can cite the relationship between money and goods and services, between threats of force and actual force, and between status symbols and recognized prestige. Governments, for example, often increase the amount of money in circulation without a parallel increase in goods and services.

An actor's power is affected by his *reputation,* which in turn is affected by how often his bluff has been effectively called. Governments which often devaluate their currency lose the confidence of users. In the area of prestige, the more symbols that are authorized (e.g., Kentucky colonelcies; dozens of vice-presidents in a corporation) the less respect they command and the less effort is expended to gain them. In politics a labor union which promises x-amount of dollars and votes but fails to produce will have greater difficulty the next time it seeks the passage of legislation.

Still, a change in the circulation of symbols does have some independent allocative effect of its own. The dilution of prestige symbols is only gradually noticed; the labor union which failed to fulfill its promises may "get by" this time. A declaration of support by n groupings may evoke others from wavering groups; this buildup may either make "cashing" unnecessary or will transform the empty promises of the initial declarations into actual commitments. The public "image," as is well-known in advertising and PR circles, can be quite influential.

All of this is possible because neither threats nor promises nor what is "delivered" are precisely measureable. Reputations for power credibility and solvency are open to manipulation. But ultimately *credibility has to be maintained or power is lost.*

Several theoreticians addressing themselves to the similarities between economic and political dynamics have not fully considered the importance of maintaining credibility, and the difference between the symbolic face and the objective base of power. Power is characterized as a "generalized symbolic medium," much like money is to the economy or language is to social action.[9] "Thus a sign, 'Beware of the dog,' may induce caution without the passerby's actual seeing or hearing a dog." True, but incomplete. If there were no dogs behind the signs (like the fabled one at Pompeii) the signs would lose their credibility; a skilled burglar is less likely to be hoodwinked. The same holds for power: Effective power is anchored in assets available for "cashing."

A subsidiary point: *Occasional* actual escalation of the degree to which threats are realized is not accidental but is inherent in the power-threat system. The more often threats are not cashed, the lower the credibility, and the higher the gains that may be made in an occasional actualization. Thus effective systems are not those that never actualize threats but those who must actualize them less often. Contrast this view with that of Neustadt that any use of force is a sign of failure.[10] As we see it, if Eisenhower in 1957 had not sent Federal troops to Little Rock, governmental capacity to gain compliance with desegregation rulings would have suffered. In international systems this symbolic use of power entails great risks. Balance-of-power theories typically allowed for "an occasional war" to restore system by punishing but not annihilating those who violated the rules of the game. Today, obviously, this is intolerable.

There are, thus, three different kinds of costs involved in the application of power: of the assets "consumed" as power is generated; of the power itself as it is spent; and of symbolic gestures which, the more often they are used, tend to hasten the point of actual expenditure. A review of these costs reinforces our point that *language is a questionable analogy for power*. Finally, it should be pointed out that the *patterns* of distribution of assets and rewards and the *dynamics* of redistribution should both be considered; we are not dealing with the allocation of a finite set of assets but rather with the reallocation of a changing total, as assets increase or decrease in the total society.

We have defined power, and argued that power is gained via *conversion* from the asset base. The power of Group A changes as its assets are withheld or committed; no group "wins them all." Power can be "stretched" by various communications, but communications unsupported by power provide no social control. Power is an inevitable component of societal control, guidance, and activeness. At the same time, power incurs a societal cost, a distorting effect which curtails activation. The next chapter pursues the various combinations of the energizing and distorting consequences of power.

NOTES

*Detailed references will be found in *The Active Society*, pp. 342–349.

1. Thucydides, *History of the Peloponnesian War*, Book 6, 24–27; 54–63.

2. Theodore R. Marmor, "Why Medicare Helped Raise Doctors' Fees," *Trans-Action*, Vol. 5 (1968), p. 17.

3. Michael Lipsky, "Protest as a Political Resource," *American Political Science Review*, Vol. 62 (1968), pp. 1144–1158.

4. *Ibid.*

5. Karl W. Deutsch, "Communication Theory and Political Integration," in Philip E. Jacob and James V. Toscano, *The Integration of Political Communities* (Philadelphia: Lippincott, 1964), p. 49.

6. Elton Mayo, *The Human Problems of an Industrial Civilization* (Boston: Division of Research, Graduate School of Business Administration, Harvard University, 1946), Ch. 8.

7. Reinhard Bendix and Lloyd H. Fisher, "The Perspectives of Elton Mayo," *Review of Economics and Statistics*, Vol. 31 (1949), pp. 312–319.

8. Thomas C. Schelling, *The Strategy of Conflict* (New York: Oxford University Press, 1963), esp. Part I.

9. Talcott Parsons, "On the Concept of Political Power," in Reinhard Bendix and Seymour M. Lipset (eds.), *Class, Status and Power* (New York: Free Press, 1966), 2nd edition, pp. 240–265.

10. Richard Neustadt, *Presidential Power* (New York: Wiley, 1960), pp. 27–28.

CHAPTER XII

Power as a Source of Alienation*

Can the self-guiding society use power to bring about its own transformation and the realization of its goals *without the "totalitarian" consequence of sacrificing commitment, participation, and legitimation?*

To use power means to generate new resistance to it. This is *the dilemma of power:* how to increase the capacity to act without generating counter-currents. Such currents may boomerang, forcing the active society to be less active, less responsive to the interests of its members.

The dilemma can never be fully resolved. The realistic question, therefore, becomes: *Which kind of power* generates the smallest counter-currents?

Social science can contribute its skills to the study of this problem. Since *power must be used,* we need to discover the kinds of power that will maximize both freedom and control, under varying conditions, with the least cost and distortion in the lives of people. To abandon the use of power in complex society is utopian and invites anarchy; the very existence of society implies a division of labor, a *differential distribution of assets and commitments,* and hence power relations. Just as the individual builds and maintains self-controls in the form of ego and superego, society too must apply controls. The question, then, turns our attention to the consequences of various kinds of power usage.

 Notes for this Chapter are on page 139.

Alienation as a Consequence of Power

The resistance generated by the use of power takes many forms, from a vague unease to sabotage. The term that most broadly describes the various kinds of resistance is "alienation." *Alienation increases when power is exercised,* adding to the alienation stemming from other sources. Alienation has both subjective and objective facets. It promotes neurosis, sullen anger, uncertainty, hopelessness, powerlessness, and the like. With such dispositions, the person tends to adapt via alcoholism, apathy, or the victimization of others (concentration-camp inmates attacked each other more than they attacked their guards). Objectively, social patterns are distorted when power is exerted: Members will show hostility toward power-wielding elites, the social world of members will be less meaningful, and the social structure will be less responsive.

Yet some form of this seemingly corrosive power is still necessary. The search for the self-guiding society entails a search for the least distorting, least alienating forms of power.

Three Forms of Social Organization

Since Hobbes in the 17th century, social scientists have asked how societies can best be organized: What kinds of glue—*or power*—could knit men into society? In the main, three organizational principles have emerged. These patterns were described in Chapter 3 as the main bases of social order.

Normative theories maintain that men are related to each other through shared emotional and moral bonds. They share a symbolic "culture," composed of values, norms (rules), and customs. This is seen most clearly in traditional, "folk" societies in which order is kept by the "natural" leadership of kinship groupings. This consensual order has been undermined by the impact of industrialization and urbanization, so that the second principle becomes relevant.

Utilitarian theories emphasize that men and groups are made interdependent by symbiotic interests rising out of the division of labor, specialization, and exchange of one good or service for another. Since this mode of organization foresees that each man or group will seek his own best interest so that the interests of all will be served, no need for overall leadership is recognized. Given the rough equality of each individual or social atom, competition for scarce resources will occur in "market" fashion (like Adam Smith's "invisible hand") to insure the good of man and society.

Countless scholars have dealt with these themes. Many have voiced a preference for normative as against utilitarian bonds. Weber saw traditional, normative authority as more stable than the rationalist, bureaucratic type. Durkheim noted that every (utilitarian) contract is based, iceberg-like, upon precontractual "customs" and understandings.[1] Since the Industrial and the French revolutions, a long line of scholars—de Toqueville, Maine, Tonnies, Redfield, and many others—have equated the weakening in the social fabric with the loss of community.[2] In the Parsonian theory of action, social organization is still rooted in the internalization by man and the institutionalization in society of normative symbols which bind units into groups. The individual "selfish" interests of men or groups may subvert the common weal.

A third set of writings, *coercive theories,* has not enjoyed such favor. Coercive relations have been widely treated as destructive. Marx believed that force was used by the propertied classes to subjugate all others; it contained, however, the seeds of its own destruction, and the old regime would be replaced by the brave new communist society, in which force has no place. Even to Hobbes it seemed that once men have accepted the absolute state, the "contract" will guide society on both normative and utilitarian terms. The use of force as an organizing principle was seen, however, by a group of Italian scholars, among whom Mosca and Pareto are the best known.

We suggest that *the three organizational principles are equal in theoretical status.* There are no grounds on which to argue that one of these serves as a more general principle than the others. Evaluation of the relative distorting effects of the three cannot be determined without relating the kind of power use to the goals served.

We will classify the kinds of power and then examine their relationship to the kinds and amounts of alienation generated, the kinds of goals sought, and to relations between the various member groups in the society. We will find, in brief, that the kind of power used is associated with different kinds of social organizations. We find three types of organization on a dimension of the kind of power employed. Actually, of course, the three principles are composites; all organizations require some amounts of normative and utilitarian controls, and all, to a greater or lesser extent, also must sometimes use force.

The Forms of Power

The conversion of assets into power generates a variety of sanctions and rewards: to *reward* those who cooperate, to *penalize* those who resist, to *remove* those who block, and to *provide facilities for* those who implement a common course of action. We suggest a threefold classification of *assets and power:* coercive, utilitarian, or persuasive.

Utilitarian assets include economic possessions, technical and administrative capabilities, manpower, and the like. When these assets are applied so that the acting unit brings other units into line, utilitarian power is being exercised. *Coercive assets* are the weapons, installations, and manpower used by military and police agencies and entail the use of force and violent means.

Persuasive power is a concept not widely used by social scientists but frequently applied in society. It is exercised through the manipulation of symbols, but only those which have already been internalized by the members. These shared symbolic values are assets for those who can appeal to them to promote a proposed program, but not for those who seek radical change. Sometimes political elites will advocate measures which raise doubts among the membership, who initially resist. Yet the program can be couched in terms of the existing value context, so that persuasive power is being used. In the 1960s the U.S. pushed for desegregation of public facilities, with equal access to be given to Negroes. Persuasive power (appealing to "the American Creed" of equality, freedom, and so on) proved fairly successful in overcoming this resistance over the years. When the issue turned to less clearly "public" facilities, however (as with the controversy over "open housing"), the latent resistance again boiled up. *Other* values (e.g. the sanctity of private property), conflicting with the humanitarian values, were expressed and used as the basis of a counter-appeal. Persuasive power thus has a structural base, in the web of shared ideas (the assets) that bind the population together. Further, it is far from being randomly distributed. A group which can count on the support of the church (e.g., Franco in the Spanish civil war) possesses a marked persuasive advantage. In democratic societies, the mass media as a source of persuasive power is more accessible to the political incumbents than to the opposition. Thus persuasive power is structured and organized, allocated and applied, in much the same way as the other two kinds of power.

Alienation in Different Compliance Structures

Basically, *the application of power has a cost,* and this cost is seen most clearly in those subject to it. We will speak of *compliance structures* as the patterns consequent to the type of power used. These structures are the relationships between the power-users and the subjects. Of the three types of power, we suggest (not surprisingly) that persuasive power is the least alienating (e.g., when the U.S. persuades a country that not trading with Cuba agrees with values that both countries share).

The application of force is probably most alienating (as when one country occupies another). In between is the use of utilitarian power (reducing the sugar quota, foreign aid). These are the three main types of compliance structures, or *the relationship between degree of power and strength of alienation.*

It is too simple to conclude, as many do, that the main source of alienation stems from the political-economic structure (expecting socialist societies to be less alienating than capitalist ones, or vice-versa), or that "modernization" generates alienation because of the rise of large-scale bureaucratization. We do believe that the shape of the distributive pattern (who gets what) and the level of responsiveness of a society are affected by the ownership of the means of production and by the complexity of social organization, and that these factors affect the level of alienation. We suggest, however, that although societies differ considerably in the general levels of alienation which they generate, there are significant differences *within* each society.

Since all societies devote portions of their activities to cultural, production, and order goals, all societies, regardless of political structure, will have some alienating and some less-alienating sectors. Thus prisoners in all societies will be alienated, students will be less so, and workers will be somewhere in between, regardless of the structure of power. Further, the type of alienation will vary between countries and between sectors—American students may condemn hypocrisy while totalitarian students bemoan lack of job freedom; and workers in different countries will voice varying kinds of complaints, from lack of consumer goods to grumbling against unresponsive government.

Power and Stratification

Many socio-political factors tend to co-vary with changes in the prevailing compliance pattern, for instance, the internal divisions of groupings and the relations among them. *Where coercion is the rule, a caste system tends to evolve.* Sharp and rigid boundaries separate the rulers from the ruled. There is little mobility between these strata and few opportunities for gradual change of status relationships; people get stuck in ruts. Such caste relationships are approximated in the relation between inmates and guards in prisons, occupation forces and native populations, and racially divided societies.

Where *normative controls* prevail, stratification will be more flat with fewer ranks, informal ranking, and mobility common. This can be seen best in social movements, especially after some success has been registered; SNCC, for example, around 1963–1965, was characterized by an insistence on the "all Indians, no generals" theme. *Utilitarian* compliance has a "middle" score, with less sharp segregation than in coercive units, more mobility, and so on, as in business corporations.

Influence

The term "authority" is usually defined as legitimate power, power used in accord with the subject's values and under conditions he views as proper. The term "influence" is sometimes equated with "power." [3] The exercise of influence entails an *authentic* change in the subject's attitudes; *he comes to agree with the influencer.* In such a case, little alienation is produced. On the other hand, when power is exercised, resistance is overcome not because the subject changes his mind, but because the objective situation has been changed and now resistance has been made more expensive, or even impossible. But the cost in alienation can be high. Of the three kinds of power, persuasive power is closest to influence, but it may produce considerable alienation in the subject. Many people, of course, have no fully developed attitude on a given point; they can be influenced to take a position by receiving new information or by being asked to "join us" by friends; or they may be given the "hard sell" by self-interested operators *and feel alienation* from such tactics.

The main point is evident: *the more alienating uses of power* have several crippling consequences. They tend to split societal units, increase the distance among the divisions, allocate rewards disproportionately to elites and "starve" the rest, increase the instrumental or manipulative orientation, and lessen the opportunity for authentic leadership and participation—in short, they *decrease the possibility of an active society.*

Power and Types of Societal Goals

Assuming that our basic proposition is valid—that normative controls incur the least cost (generate the least alienation and resistance), the question arises: What prevents societal units from limiting their projects to those on which there is a consensus, or to those which can be guided by normative controls? *The limits are inherent in the kinds of goals served,* since the goals differ in their ability to rely on the three major kinds of power.

Cultural (or symbolic) goals are, it seems, most readily implemented by normative controls. If the goal is education, socialization, rehabilitation, the reinforcement of normative commitments, or tension release (as in entertainment), *little other power is needed, and alienation is low.* Interestingly, when other kinds of power are employed to advance cultural goals, alienation rises and effectiveness is reduced. Paying children to be socialized generates a calculative orientation which undermines identification with the agents of socialization, and thus a prime mechanism is lost. Force weakens rehabilitation efforts. When such efforts do succeed, they follow or are accompanied by a reduction in the use of force.

Production goals are served more effectively by utilitarian power. Production (of goods and services) is a "rational" activity, requiring specialization, control, and coordination. Therefore it requires rewards that can be allocated in close association with performance. *Coercion will fail* because most kinds of work require some degree of initiative, responsibility, and commitment, even for the rank and file. Only routine "gang" work, such as carrying loads or rowing in triremes, can be well controlled by coercion. Symbolic rewards are adequate for intermittent work, especially the dramatic kind such as flood and fire brigades or rescue operations. Nursing shifted from normative to utilitarian as it left its Florence Nightingale days and became a bureaucratically organized profession.[4] A comparison of peacetime armies with combat troops further highlights the point: Utilitarian control is much more likely in the routine situation.

Order goals involve the control of deviants by segregating them from society and punishing them. Thus most prisons see their mission as protecting society from their charges and tend to fall back on coercive controls. It is no accident, thus, that rehabilitation is a secondary aim and is poorly achieved.

Post-Modern Trends in Work

The post-modern world appears to be turning to the less alienating means of control. In shops, offices, schools, and correctional institutions, the shift away from coercive strait-jacketing can be found—although no conclusions should be drawn until more evidence is available.

Work patterns change strikingly as we move into the post-modern world. On the average, work is less routine and less supervised and demands more skill, initiative, and responsibility. More routine work is automated: Fewer jobs remain in blue-collar categories. Thus on the whole work should yield less alienating compliance patterns. Related trends are the rise in productivity, due chiefly to more efficient technology, the widespread increase in education, the rise in the average age of first employment, somewhat shorter hours, more vacation time, and the increased education of women. Before these trends of changes in compliance can reduce alienation, however, the legitimacy of non-work and the value of cultural activities must continue to be more widely recognized.

This compliance shift must not be oversimplified. Cybernation does not always reduce routine labor (for example it demands temporarily an increased need for card punchers). It can also increase centralization. Further, some workers prefer routine, psychologically non-demanding employment,[5] and some prefer directive to non-directive supervision.[6] Thus a coming problem is to make the job and the worker's preferences more congruent, if we are to continue modifying alienation without sacrificing productivity.

We have suggested that control of post-modern work could be, on the average, less bureaucratic and more self-guiding. This is already seen in the growing symbolization of society and the greater number of professional jobs—in education, R&D, the helping professions, the mass media. But management and labor organizations will have to cooperate in institutional reforms. So far, most labor unions—a major potential source of such mobilization—have shown little understanding of the post-modern world. They continue to focus upon *utilitarian rather than normative* matters. The few unions and labor parties showing a broader political concern tend to be obsolescent, seeking to combat alienation either by substituting the bureaucracy of the state for that of the corporation or by promoting more welfare legislation. Both of these are chiefly utilitarian alternatives.

Away from Alienating Forms of Power

Modern societies have tended to suppress the use of mass violence within their own domain and have externalized it, raising the "we" feeling to the national level and projecting the negative "they" on other countries. The reduction of this warlike violence, we suggest, requires the evolution of integrative bonds among societies just as they previously evolved among what are now integral parts of the same society (e.g., among the German states).

Within post-modern society, we expect continued transformation of the control of deviants from custodial (coercive) toward more therapeutic (normative) patterns, a trend which began in the modern period. Deviants will be treated as if they had insufficient opportunity for socialization and will receive that chance. Other deviations will come to be defined as tolerable; the new view toward homosexuality and some forms of drug intake in Scandinavia and Britain have been showing the way. About half the crimes in New York City are committed by addicts who must purchase their drugs illegally and at high prices. Were drugs available under supervision of medical and public authorities (as in Britain[7]), much of this crime could disappear. This type of transformation is already seen with respect to the treatment of mental patients—more therapeutic, less custodial.

Another shift in power toward normative primacy has commenced with new awareness of threats in the areas of ecology and birth control. Even economic giants like General Motors recognize universal needs for pure air. The issue becomes sharpest when common resources are destroyed: upper-class residents of Santa Barbara turned into radical activists against the oil companies when channel oil spills blackened their sunny beaches.[8]

Twentieth century trends have turned away from coercion, toward more utilitarian and especially normative compliance. The more active a society, the more this trend will continue. There is a double gain: The lower level of alienation makes the society more responsive and more effective, so that compliance structures are even less alienating, and the level of resentment and resistance continues to drop. Each of these statements should be seen as hypothesis rather than fact—but there are some data to document each. They are optimistic, but this should not invalidate them as scientific points of departure for research. Pessimistic predictions, of course, are also legitimate. Which outcome will occur depends to a significant degree on the scope of social mobilization, responsiveness, community-building, and the reduction of inauthenticity—factors to which we now turn.

NOTES

*Detailed references will be found in *The Active Society*, pp. 381–386.

1. Emile Durkheim, *The Division of Labor in Society* (New York: Macmillan, 1933), pp. 206–219.

2. Robert Nisbet, *The Sociological Tradition* (New York: Basic Books, 1966).

3. For a detailed discussion of influence and power as they relate to social control, see William A. Gamson, *Power and Discontent* (Homewood, Ill.: Dorsey, 1968).

4. William A. Glaser, "Nursing Leadership and Policy: Some Cross-National Comparisons," in Fred Davis (ed.), *The Nursing Profession* (New York: Wiley & Sons, 1966), pp. 1–25, 43–45.

5. Charles R. Walker and Robert H. Guest, *The Man on the Assembly Line* (Cambridge, Mass: Harvard University Press, 1952), pp. 52–56, 62, 145.

6. Rensis Likert, *New Patterns of Management* (New York: McGraw-Hill, 1961), esp. pp. 5–60.

7. Edwin M. Schur, *Narcotic Addiction in Britain and America* (Bloomington, Ind.: Indiana University Press, 1962).

8. Harvey Molotch, "Santa Barbara: Oil in the Velvet Playground," *Ramparts*, Vol. 8 (November, 1969), pp. 43–51.

CHAPTER XIII

Societal Mobilization and Change*

Much of history is epitomized in the *rise of new groups to power*. These groups have successfully "mobilized," meaning that they have *committed* a high level of their assets, members, and attention to the pursuit of collective goals. In this chapter our question is: Under what conditions is this commitment and mobilization high or low, rising or falling?

Mobilization is the process by which latent assets are committed to group control and use. It resembles a campaign or drive, and is at least in part deliberately initiated and directed rather than being a chance byproduct of conventional exchanges. It answers the question, "What is the source of energy for societal action?" When a group mobilizes, energy already present but "in suspension" is marshalled for active duty. With added mobilization, a group can accomplish more either by increasing the number of goals it reaches or by heightening the intensity of its pursuit of those goals. People, money, time, equipment—all such assets are converted from private control to the beck of the group. *The rise in the capacity to control and use assets* is the nub of the idea.

Depending on the kind of assets involved, mobilization is *coercive* (as when feudal lords turn their armies over to the king), *utilitarian* (a state raises the level of taxation), or *normative* (loyalties to the nation are increased, while those to local communities decline).

Mobilization is generally initiated and directed by elites, whose power is proportionately increased. It is a *downward* process and thus has a cost. When the direction, scope, and

 Notes for this Chapter are on pages 153 and 154.

intensity of mobilization clash with what is legitimate for and supported by the evolving *consensus, mobilization generates alienation* in the same way as other exercises of power.

The term was first used to describe the "draft," the shifting of resources from civilian to military control. More recently the term has connoted a group's deliberate increase in the control of assets, such as a new nation's mobilization of economic resources for development or a civil rights movement's mobilization of the loyalty of previously passive citizens.

It is relatively easy to *measure* coercive mobilization (changes in the control over troops, arms, and the like) and utilitarian mobilization. Examples of the latter are the percentage of the GNP taxed by all levels of government and the distribution of these funds among them or the ratio of people employed by the federal government to those employed by state and local governments. It is somewhat more difficult to measure normative mobilization, although changes in sentiments expressed in opinion polls or changes in the frequency of various symbols in the press have been used as rough measures.[1]

Changing Social Structures

The theory of societal guidance differs most from other theories in that it sees the mobilization drives of groups and societies as *a major source of their own transformations.* If people are dissatisfied they can do nothing, grumble, or move toward change. As a unit mobilizes, its own structure tends to change, and the structure of its supra-unit as well. For example, the drive of West European nations to overcome the depleting effects of World War II brought both internal transformation (in favor of the center parties) and the formation of a trans-national community. De-Stalinization, a process of demobilization, altered the internal structures of East European communist societies, and also deunified the bloc.[2]

There are, of course, other sources of social change. There

are technology, the role of new ideas, changes in the means of production, migration, and so on. But these tend to establish the *conditions* which provide the prerequisites for increases in the unit's activities. Mobilization, in contrast, is the drive by which potentials are directly moved toward actualization.

Marx argued that history is propelled by *class* struggles. We hold that the acting units are often *collectivities* whose primary base is not shared economic interests but *shared values and statuses,* especially ethnic ones—and that group relationships are not always "struggles" but various mixes of conflict *and* cooperation. The process occurs between the mobilizers and the unmobilized in one and the same group or society. Were all the members to rally all their assets toward a given goal, it would be as if all the latent energy locked in a pound of material were released and transformed into power. It would promote high levels of activeness and would alter the social map.

Thus mobilization is a steering process. It activates and guides. The process entails a shift of control and/or a shift in the usage of assets. *With mobilization a unit becomes less private, more public, more politically intensive.* For example, to the degree that corporations follow government-set guidelines—perhaps as to price increases—a gain in the national level of mobilization is achieved. Or, more indirectly, by issuing large sums of money (i.e., by generating an inflation), a state can gain control of the assets of some members (such as those whose incomes are fixed) without legislation, fiat, or even without inviting cooperation.

The Opportunities of Crisis

It is *during a crisis* that mobilization expands most sharply. Natural disasters—tornadoes, floods, and the like—call forth widespread volunteer aid. Conventional tasks are set aside and large networks of public assistance appear. In the pre-mobilization days of the mid-1950s, the civil rights movement in Chicago could not raise $10,000 for the Urban League, and NAACP meetings were attended by fewer than 50 people.[3] During the crisis of 1966–1967, much larger amounts of money and manpower became available.[4] During the bombing of Tokyo in 1944–1945, thousands of city blocks had their block wardens and crews ready for immediate duty; mobilization approached the maximum. Similar attempts to organize New York City in 1942 failed; there was no visible crisis from Nazi attacks.

Crisis *threatens* the group with obliteration, marked shifts in structure, or severely reduced assets—perhaps all three. Faced with such dire futures, members become less reluctant to step forward and take on new tasks. Crisis brings events and conditions that require action, merely to survive. Thus the depression and widespread unemployment forced the mobilization in 1933 of officials, lawyers, labor leaders, intellectuals, and social workers into "New Deal" rounds of legislation and related actions.

While crisis-mobilization is great in comparison to conventional times, it should be emphasized that *even in crisis* the level of mobilization tends not to be high in the absolute sense. Thus even if mobilization in a crisis triples the amount of social energy, still no more than a third of the potential assets, manpower, and attention of the members may actually be mobilized. Often the fraction is smaller. From 1961 to 1965 the civil rights movement was joined by college students from the North, but not more than 5000 students out of some 5,000,000 were involved. And the student New Left, in the later 1960s, which initiated the anti-war movement and changed university structure, measured less than 4 per cent. The French Revolution was launched by as many as 80,000 persons (the second invasion of the Tuilleries; the march on Versailles); only about 800 or 900 stormed the Bastille.[5]

It appears that in crises, major social changes are propelled by small shifts in the absolute level of mobilization because they constitute sharp increases in the *relative* pool of energy available. Thus without approaching a level even approximating full mobilization, there seems to be considerable leeway for a higher level of push.

The main questions for the transformation toward an active society are: Can it be achieved in non-crisis situations? Can it be done for internal, self-transformations instead of aggression against other societies (e.g., Nazi Germany)? Can it be done without generating so much alienation that consensus disappears? In short, is a "permanent revolution," a continual and authentic self-guiding society, possible? To these massive questions we have no answer, but events of the 1970s and 1980s should provide considerably more insight than we command today.

The Beginnings of Mobilization

How does mobilization start? How does it evolve and mature? In any society, a few units are already mobilized and may even reach the point of "ceiling effects." Of much more interest is the mobilization of the more typical groupings, not yet activated.

Predisposing factors, stressed in the collectivistic approach, include rising levels of income and education in the previous decades, with perhaps an interruption of these gains shortly before agitation as a triggering factor. The presence of external elites often becomes an activating force: intellectuals, students, and clergy have served as catalytic agents. Beyond this, the crucial sparking input is the personal or collective project. *The project* supplies the internal stimulus, followed by a slow chain-reaction energizing one group after another, guided by internal leadership.

The approach we use is the accumulation or "value-added" model.[6] We first discuss the factor which initiates a large number of processes. From each start, some groups take off, others do not. For those that do, we ask, What is added? Then we proceed to analyze the increment in the next inning, and so on. A full analysis would also investigate the causes of failures to start at all, the source of halting activation, and so on. The successful movements are treated like a Guttman scale, in that if the later factors are present, the earlier ones are expected to be present also.

THE PROJECT

The take-off stage of an internal mobilization is often marked by increasing numbers of collective projects. *A project is a concerted campaign entailing the focusing of energy with intensive and guided activity striving toward specific goals.* A community may establish a day-care center so that mothers can work; later, the center may be expanded into a co-op. At each period value is added. Projects spur mobilization because they release hitherto latent energy. The Montgomery bus boycott, the Boston Tea Party, and the building of the Parthenon were typical projects.

The importance of projects is that they, like other catalytic agents, may release much more energy than they themselves can use or command. This considerable power is "catalytic" for two reasons. First, the "walls" which theretofore prevented mobilizing may be psychological, and the projects which test them may show their mythicality. A vacuum emerges, and energy can flow into it via the new project. Or the walls may stand, but are less than formidable; a "Jericho" blast may raze them. Second, the constraints may in fact be real, but a project may launch the group into efforts that add new value to their strength so that further mobilization will permit a fair contest. Not all projects, of course, succeed, but their potential in mobilization cannot be overestimated.

Historians often commence their accounts with the very first idea or cell which seeded the movement in an earlier time. But because so many of these have aborted, we start with the project stage, which indicates the presence of elites nourishing ideas with some chance of stirring change. Although encompassing mobilization is still far from inevitable, projects raise the chances.

Projects leading to mobilization take-offs may occur within groups or around the total society. Whereas the going is slower in the former—much organizing work being required—the point of origin is often startlingly clear in the case of societies. Pearl Harbor, for example, or the 1948 Communist coup in Czechoslovakia which sent western nations into the formation of NATO —these were *single events* which impelled mobilization. Even a group-based process may commence with a single event, an example being Rosa Parks' refusal to move to the rear of a bus, thus launching the Montgomery bus boycott and—to use hindsight—the civil rights movement.

Projects generate internal change in the mobilizing units; they call forth new personal and collective *commitments.*[7] One way to commit a person is to get him to act, to participate; later, he may go from signing a petition to carrying a sign, from boycotting a shop to marching in a demonstration. His "political map" expands, he may shift resources from personal to group use; he spends less time watching television, more with the movement. His self-awareness expands; he gains a new vision of his own potential; he acquires a new self-image. In mixing with others who are joining the project, he finds new role models and starts to define himself as an activist. Commitment seems to spur more commitment, more feeling of excitement, more interaction with fellow activists, and less of the earlier pattern of privatization. In the individual, commitment means "I care"; it is the opposite of alienation.

Scores of "poverty projects" mushroomed in American cities during the 1960s. Leadership came from universities, from the black community, from the church, and from other organizations, such as Saul Alinsky's Industrial Areas Foundation.[8] Funding was supplied mostly by the federal government. They won a number of long-overdue concessions—rat removal, housing repair, welfare services, police protection, voting rights, and so on. But the establishment and apathy balked fundamental transformations; the changes proved mostly local and particularistic. Poor people did perceive, however, that action was possible, and communities gained greater awareness of festering conditions. As to tactics, one study concluded that militant "social action" scored fewer gains than the milder and more classical community development techniques.[9]

PROBLEMS WITH PROJECTS

While projects are a nucleus for initiating mobilization, they often fail to become encompassing (the poverty projects) and thus fail to bring fundamental change. Often, in fact, they catch fire slowly, burn fitfully, and die out, whereupon mobilization returns to the old level.

In the more successful cases, the process follows a pattern of a slow *chain reaction.* Some units are more active than others; some take years to warm up while a few are crackling and the rest remain dormant. For instance, only a few student bodies of the 2000 colleges and universities in the U.S. followed the 1964 Free Speech Movement at Berkeley with similar movements; another few launched smaller projects, more commenced to examine student-faculty relations, several hundred devoted increased attention to the issue, and the remainder were barely affected. A second round, more encompassing than the first, followed the Columbia riots of 1968.

Many questions remain to be explored. (This is not the place to discuss the advisability of various *tactics* for group activism, such as how to organize a community, staff an agency, or write publicity; many groups prepare their own guidelines, and some are published.) But which elites and units are mobilized earlier, which later? What is the value to a movement of a successful model as catalyst and inspiration to the fence-sitting majority? In which situations does the progress advance rather than exhaust itself? What encourages backlash? Should group leaders sponsor mobilization when "public opinion" clearly rejects the aims of the movement? Or should they build a firm base gradually, or shift goals diagonally, to avoid the head-on confrontation with power? Does one gain by attacking obsolescent sacred cows frontally, or indirectly? When will "creative tension," as used by Martin Luther King, be most effective in a community crisis? Such questions indicate that organizational and symbolic strategies of the chain reaction remain to be explored. No formula or magic wand stipulates tactics for all movements.

It follows from the above that we expect *mobilization to be an elitist process.* There is not one elite and one mass of followers, but rather several elites, semi-elites, and various subgroups activated to varying degrees, as well as segments of passive sympathizers, onlookers, and occasional contributors.

Within any given unit, its capacity to act and its historical impact depends on the outcome of the struggle between the mobilizers and the parts that lag.[10] Its "uprising" usually follows long periods of effort during which an internal leadership slowly forms. Even at the end of this process, the attention, loyalties, and utilitarian assets of the members are *unevenly tapped.* Mobilization slowly penetrates from one layer to another, rarely embracing all of them or moving very rapidly because of this internal struggle. Some elements resist out of principle, others shy at diverting assets to the cause; differences over means, pace, tactics, and leadership afflict and divide the group. Such differences can be resolved in part by consensus-formation mechanisms, in part only by the exercise of power by elites. And of course many units expend greater efforts in times of crisis, but not all. Even studies of struggles for national independence reveal some groupings contributing little or nothing to the anti-colonial movement.

Organizations as the Engine of Mobilization

Organizations are a major tool of the process of mobilization. The elites of organizations, their power hierarchies and communication networks, are usually the most mobilized subunit of a grouping (the main exceptions being in mass movements). Thus the act of organizing brings an increase in the level of mobilization, as seen in the launching of new labor unions or the political arms of church or youth groups.

Rarely is the mobilization of a grouping controlled by one organization (although a society is frequently mobilized by one state). Usually, initial mobilization is carried out by *two or more organizations.* While this may sound wasteful, especially if the two groups do not see eye-to-eye with each other, the two groups draw support from different recruitment bases, in terms of age, education level, past affiliations, and so on. Oddly enough, *this seeming split adds strength to the movement.* This point is seldom discussed, and when it is, the internal strains between the two groups receive the attention of observers. Sociologically, this jockeying should be expected; it is illustrated by the division of labor between the NAACP and the Urban League in early civil rights work. The former was more politically oriented, the latter stressed jobs and social work. The two groups were joined in the 1960s by a host of pro-Negro organizations, each working more or less by itself and joining in coalitions only around major pushes. Some persons will join because of an ideological orientation, some will seek thrills, and others will attach themselves to less demanding groups in search of friendly interpersonal contacts. Groups organized by Saul Alinsky, for example, appealed to militants, while more conventional groups continued to work in the same community.[11]

Multi-organization mobilization tends to *draw the teeth of counter-mobilization.* As one of many examples, consider the British in the 1940s facing not one but two major underground groups in Palestine. *Hagana* was broadly based and moderate, *Irgun* was narrowly based and militant. The two organizations were in conflict, sometimes to the point of informing on the other to the British. Many sympathizers, appalled at the cost, strove to unite the two groups. Yet in retrospect, it appears that the split strengthened the Israeli side. World public opinion supported *Hagana.* When *Irgun* engaged in an "extremist" act which invited massive British retaliation, *Irgun* members hid in the community at large, which had *Hagana* sympathies. With few exceptions the British found it difficult and politically unwise (because of world opinion) to institute harsh police measures against the entire community.

In short, the generally low level of mobilization, its slow and uneven (often elitist) nature, and the functional aspects of interorganizational diversity, strain, and conflict seem to be *three universal features of the mobilization of social movements.*

The Role of Stratification

Mobilization is closely related to stratification. Active members are more often found in the higher classes. From 5 to perhaps 30 per cent of the American public are active in political life (depending whether the criterion is contributing money and time to campaigns, displaying buttons or stickers, or talking about their candidates to others), and few of these are in the lower classes.[12] Being high in status, and to gain a greater level of consciousness, an individual or group tends to be more directly in command of assets. High position also may permit the group to constrain the mobilization of lower groups, whether by diverting them, co-opting their leaders, or harassing their organizers, as in the case of early union history and recent Negro movements in the Deep South.

There is a tendency to view stratification position as a cause and the level of mobilization (or capacity to mobilize) as resulting from it.[13] In contrast, we wish to stress the *interaction effect* of the two factors. This effect is clear *when previously disadvantaged groups rise.* They had occupied a low position, along with other groups, but their mobilization has improved their class position as contrasted to non-mobilized groups. Further, the level of mobilization can be *increased* before a significant change in class position occurs.

In general, mobilization is more likely to be initiated if one or more of these conditions is met: (1) if a stratification imbalance has been created due to an increase one kind of assets but not in other kinds (as with income vs. prestige among the *nouveau riche*); (2) if a decrease in any kind of assets has occurred (downward mobility as among small businessmen vs.

large corporation executives); and (3) when external elites help in the organizing (middle-class leaders of early labor movements).

Counter-Mobilization and Third Parties

Since mobilization changes a group, it also may change its relationships with other groups. These other groups include competitors, allies, and the mobilized group's supra-unit.

Counter-mobilization is often spurred when a competing unit mobilizes, in order that the unit's gain may be neutralized. In the arms race starting in 1947, the U.S. and Russia continually counter-mobilized each other, fostering an upward-spiralling arms race. A California poll after 1964 showed that 92 per cent of the public was aware of student demonstrations at Berkeley, a remarkably high proportion; yet most of this new attention proved to be potential counter-mobilization, as 74 per cent expressed disapproval of the demonstrations.[14] In southern states in the years following the 1954 desegregation decision, announced activities by pro-integration forces would set off much greater blasts from the white citizens' councils.

Often, as in the above example, such contests are characterized by the presence of "third parties," uncommitted units but potential allies. They may be weak (a "floating" vote from some quarter as seen in many democratic elections), or strong (the U.S. and the U.S.S.R. in conflicts between Israel and the Arab states and between India and Pakistan). They may be from business or labor, a church or woman's organization, or from any quarter at all. Allies certainly add strength, but further questions must be asked as to concessions gained and risks taken vis-á-vis still other units: Does the ally's aid to unit X jeopardize its relations with unit Y?

When a mobilizing group is challenging the elite structure of its own society, *premature* attempts at a coup are often observed. The group is poorly organized, has poor societal knowledge, and underestimates the power needed to supplant the ruling elite. Example: 1905 may be viewed as a "trial run" for the Russian Revolution.

Thus, from the viewpoint of each grouping, its mobilization efforts and the external constraints upon them affect each other. Mobilization finds and uses whatever options the total structure allows for changing it, and changing the structure can expand these options. Thus, the mobilization of Negroes in the sit-ins starting in 1960 led to some reallocation of utilitarian assets, greatly expanded public awareness (and growing sympathy), increased political representation, and so on, which, in turn, improved the conditions for further mobilization and further projects.

The Approach of Guidance and Process

Our thesis is that (1) much can be gained by the self-mobilization of an actor and by the mobilization of others' support, and that (2) the actor's capacity to be mobilized and to mobilize others is determined by external factors to a lesser extent than is often assumed. Projects, starting well inside a group with "dawning awareness," can trigger a chain reaction and lead a group to many new options. These in turn may loosen the age-old social constraints on the group, make gains more possible, and so on to further transformation. In the late 1960s, for example, a vast "new working class"—composed of the poor and welfare groups—was envisioned as being poised for mobilization.[15] Counter-mobilization began to rise from "the silent majority" above them.

The theory of societal guidance outlined here differs from functionalist theories not only in its greater concern with *transformation as a process* but also in its concern with the *sources of change*—with assets, power, energy, commitment, mobilization. It is not enough to take a "cultural" viewpoint by specifying the norms which characterize a new pattern—that, for example, "achievement-orientation" is required for modernization (or universalism, specificity, or neutrality).[16] We are interested in *how* the achievement-oriented groups strive for power—and that has been the topic of this chapter.

From the viewpoint of the entire society, rather than that of rising groups, we also need to know how the many groups in the society come to agree on a set of specific programs to seek their goals. This is the topic of consensus-formation, and it is our next subject.

NOTES

*Detailed references will be found in *The Active Society,* pp. 422–427.

1. Quincy Wright, *A Study of War* (Chicago: University of Chicago Press, 1965), pp. 1448–1458.

2. Zbigniew K. Brzezinski, *The Soviet Bloc: Unity and Conflict,* rev. ed. (New York: Praeger, 1961), pp. 157–181.

3. James Q. Wilson, *Negro Politics: The Search for Leadership* (New York: Free Press, 1960), pp. 4–5.

4. *New York Times,* April 30, 1967.

5. George Rudé, *The Crowd in the French Revolution* (Oxford: Oxford University Press, 1959), pp. 56, 76, 89, 153–154.

6. Neil Smelser, *Theory of Collective Behavior* (New York: Free Press, 1963).

7. For individual cases of persons becoming active in movements, see Kenneth Keniston, *The Young Radicals* (New York: Harcourt, Brace and World, 1968), and Robert Coles and Joseph Brenner, "American Youth in a Social Struggle," *American Journal of Orthopsychiatry,* Vol. 35 (1965), pp. 909–926.

8. Warner Bloomberg Jr. and Florence W. Rosenstock, "Who Can Activate the Poor?", in Bloomberg and Schmandt, *Power, Poverty and Urban Policy* (Beverly Hills: Sage, 1968), Chap. 11.

9. *Ibid.*

10. For an example, see George Brager, "Organizing the Unaffiliated in a Low-Income Area," in Mayer N. Zald (ed.), *Social Welfare Institutions* (New York: Wiley, 1965), pp. 646–648.

11. Frank Riessman, "Self-Help Among the Poor," *Trans-Action,* Vol. 2 (1965), pp. 32–37.

12. Lester Milbrath, *Political Participation* (Chicago: Rand McNally, 1965), p. 19.

13. See, for example, Kenneth B. Clark, *Dark Ghetto* (New York: Harper & Row, 1965), p. 27.

14. Colin Miller, "The Press and the Student Revolt," in Michael V. Miller and Susan Gilmore (eds.), *Revolution at Berkeley* (New York: Dial Press, 1965), p. 347.

15. S. M. Miller and Frank Riessman, *Social Class and Social Policy* (New York: Basic Books, 1968). Many others have discussed these move-

ments; see, e.g., Henry Etzkowitz and Gerald M. Schlaflander, "A Manifesto for Sociologists: Institution-Formation—A New Sociology," *Social Problems,* Vol. 15 (1968), pp. 399–408.

16. The norms are those, of course, of Parsons' "pattern variables." For their application to modernization, see David McClelland, *The Achieving Society* (Princeton: Princeton University Press, 1961).

PART IV

SOCIETAL CONSENSUS AND RESPONSIVENESS

CHAPTER XIV

The Bases of Consensus in Society*

Most societies fail to reach their goals or solve their problems. Their generally low capacity to guide social processes can be traced, most basically, to *two major kinds of limitations:* to *deficiences in control processes,* which we have been discussing, and to the *lack of consensus,* to which we now turn our attention.

Marxists say that the idea of consensus conceals the fact that conflict is the basis of society. The social will, they maintain, is the will of the powerful exploiting the weak. While we agree that conflict is basic to social life and that consensus reflects the will of some more than of others, *many systems do develop a shared pattern;* conflict may occur around this pattern, but it is a shared one nonetheless. *Strong societies have mechanisms which produce,* from the disparate wills of their members, *a shared will which does reflect the interests of its members.* An authentic consensus will be discussed in chapters 17, 18, and 19.

In this chapter we look at the social organization of modern societies, in terms of their crucial social units. Are they *individuals* whose preferences are tallied via market and voting mechanisms to provide consensus? Are they powerful *elites* who impose their "consensus?" Or is the society a *network of collective bonds and links* which use both the "downward" means of control and the "upward" means of expressing preferences? This is a main question of the chapter. It introduces a following question: Are the demands of the various groupings not incompatible?

Notes for this Chapter are on page 166.

We disagree with the Marxists here; we hold that to the degree that a society can act in unison at all, it has some mechanisms for converting the several demands of its members into collective policy. We add that social goals may be achieved when various members have incompatible demands *so long as the society is responsive to the needs of the membership at large, and not just those of a minority.* We approach the problem of consensus-formation by studying first the organization of modern society.

The Theory of "Mass Society"

Modern societies, whether democratic or totalitarian, are often depicted rather loosely as "mass society."[1] This picture argues that elites manipulate individual persons directly, using charismatic appeal and the mass media. Individuals, in their turn, respond directly to the leaders who control them, like puppets on a string. There is a one-way flow of influence, all downward from elites to "the masses." "Democracy," in the sense of citizen responsibility and autonomy, is therefore a sham.

We reject this view, for modern pluralistic societies and for most totalitarian societies as well. Instead, we point to the existence of a set of "intermediate groupings" which mediate between elites and individual persons. Elites do have access to the ears of citizens, but it is indirect, being filtered through the groupings. And citizens have access to the elites, through their membership in groups which may exert pressure upon the elites, using propaganda, lobbying, the appeal to normative values, and utilitarian devices (e.g., exchanging concessions for support - "votes").[2]

The difference between these two views may be suggested by a homely analogy. The mass society view can be likened to rain falling on a bed of sand; droplets move directly downward to and past each individual grain. Our view takes rather the form of a conglomerate cube, composed variously of mud, pebbles, sand, stones, and shale, the whole being intertwined with roots, grasses and reeds. Drops of water cannot penetrate unchecked through all these intermediate layers and groupings; some are captured by this or that bloc. Further, there is a two-way flow; some of the moisture travels back up, via the root systems. The latter picture we see as a more accurate representation of the structure of modern political society.

It is true that isolated persons, like grains of sand, can be found in modern societies, especially in the lower class.[3] This "masslike" population is often concentrated in the run-down areas of central cities: the ethnic minorities, the old and left-behind, the handicapped, the recent in-migrant, the divorced, and the alcoholic, the addict, the crotchety, and the ill-educated lower classes who cannot or will not play roles more congenial to the community. Meanwhile most of the millions of people around them belong to collectivities.

"Mass society" theory goes back to the two explosive revolutions, the French and the Industrial. Following these great wrenchings, a series of writers have lamented "the erosion of community"—the weakening of family, village, church, guild, and other cohesion-maintaining social units. These units were felt to be disintegrating, thus setting the individual man on a new and lonely course.

Group Functions Not Lost, But Changed

This drastic atomization of society has not come about. Rather, these cohesive groups have *changed their functions*. The family, for example, no longer a unit of economic production, is more of a child-raising and companionship group.[4] The church, in fact, is often criticized for being "too social," rather than stressing worship. Work groups, while usually not the close-knit "cells" some observers like Durkheim have called for, often provide expressive settings for friendly fellowship.

In the process of transformation, the internal structure of many groupings has become less hierarchical and less authoritarian, and membership has become less ascribed, more open. As a result the groups seem to be more responsive to their members. One finds a greater tolerance for admission into religious and other groups. Together with this increased inclusiveness, the greater mobility—both horizontal and vertical—required by post-modern societies actually *increases the options* of urban persons to choose the groups most compatible to them. In addition, new kinds of groups have emerged, some of which are mainly expressive (social clubs) and some of which are highly achievement-oriented (occupational, business, and professional associations).

A further note about the relationship between the person and modern society revolves around the lesser scope and pervasiveness of organizations. Whereas older societies knew fewer associations, they contained larger proportions of the population and imposed upon them similar sets of norms. Today the average individual plays numerous roles and is thus a member of several groupings, none of which can choke him with overweening constraint.

Fewer organizations today straitjacket their members; few can "deliver" the vote of all members. Thus modern man is fragmented, but this not only leads to dilemmas of role conflict from time to time; it also increases his autonomy and freedom.[5] (At least his potential freedom; many people, of course, do not seize and utilize their freedoms.)

Key Groups: Collectivities and Organizations

Having argued that modern society is no "ant-hill" of atomized individuals, we now examine the groups men form and the ways in which these groups provide an "upward" expression of their interests, to the elites and to the state. Our first point is that these groups are not equal in size and importance, as a quick reading of "pluralist" theory might suggest. The most crucial types of groups are the *organization,* the "action arm" of mobilization, and the *collectivity.* It is through these groups that men who share perspectives can bring their views to the attention of those in power.

GROUPS: EXPRESSIVE AND ACTIVE

These groupings were discussed in Chapter 3. The *collectivity* is larger than an organization but smaller than a society, has great action potential, and is based on the shared normative interests of its members. Examples are American Negroes, the working class, and entrepreneurs with a Protestant orientation. We see the collectivity as more crucial than the Marxist "class" or the pluralist "veto-group" in political mobilization and consensus-formation.

The collectivities are "fed" by *sub-collectivities,* which are smaller and are typically ecologically concentrated (especially lower-class ones). They are more expressive than administrative or action-oriented, being an existing pattern of associational activities, symbolization, and integration. An example would be upper east side New York Reform Jews. Their normative solidarity builds from one or more of their facets—cultural, ethnic, religious, or economic. Finally, these somewhat amorphous groupings, to be effective, must be activated by *organizations*—action-oriented groups which mobilize assets into power in the political arena. Examples are political parties, trade unions, and groups like CORE and SDS; they are often studied as "pressure groups."

We hold that the collectivity performs a dual function: it is *"defensive" in protecting the individual member from penetration by state elites, and it is "offensive" in expressing the members' views upward to elites.* The collectivity's strength stems from its size and solidarity; being anchored in organizations and sub-collectivities in which members know each other, it has a stability and reality which add to its capacity to act in unison over periods of time, but especially when its values are threatened.

This strength is recognized by the state and societal elites. We suggest that the state and, more generally, the political processes deal much more with organizations that represent sub-collectivities and their combinations than with organizations which have no collective base. The state deals *directly* with individuals mostly in limited periods of sharp transition in which the "mass" element is pronounced (e.g., Germany in the early 1930s or Russia in 1916–1917). During such times, the collectivities remain but are out of phase with the national polity. Transformations may occur in such times. These periods, moreover, tend to generate a quick counter-action to the "mass" situation; social movements rise to mobilize commitments and redouble activations. Thus society seems to abhor the "mass" situation—to avoid it most of the time and retreat from it rapidly when it arises.

Most political sociology fails to recognize these post-Marxian features and the action potential residing within groups of solidary sub-collectivities waiting to be mobilized.

Relationships Between Groups and the State

If all modern societies contain similar building-stones in the form of groupings, *the way these groupings are combined into supra-units* differs considerably. These differences influence *how active* the society will be—and how autonomous, authentic, and consensual. *The two main dimensions* along which societies differ are those of *degree of specification by the state and degree of penetration by the state.* We shall examine these in turn.

Totalitarian states use *prescriptive control* over member units. Man's conduct is directed specifically—what to do, what not to do. (The word "total" in totalitarian suggests the *range* of conduct—including personal and family affairs—the state can specify.) The party-state controls, adapts, and transforms any unit under its prescriptive control. The degree differs between societies: The Soviet Union is more prescriptive than Poland, but Khrushchev's Russia was less prescriptive than Stalin's. Even the less specifically controlled totalitarian societies (e.g., Tito's Yugoslavia) are still more prescriptive than the more specifically controlled democracies (e.g., deGaulle's France.)

Democratic societies fall toward the opposite pole: *contextuating* control sets the *limits within which* those who are subject to control are *free to alter their conduct and make their own decisions.* For example, the Federal Communications Commission (FCC) does not tell a TV station what to broadcast and what not to broadcast; it merely formulates guidelines and occasionally monitors programming. The various groupings interact with each other and with the state *within an overall context* set by all units. Normative bonds and utilitarian links between the groupings promote a given degree of cohesion in the larger society. Each group is relatively autonomous, insulated from manipulation by external elites; and each has some capacity to mobilize, bring change and possible transformation.

PENETRATION OF GROUPS BY THE STATE

The second dimension in the relationship between group and state is the *degree of penetration of groups* by the state. The form of penetration is *usually indirect.* Cases of *direct* penetration by the state tend to be so costly as to be self-defeating. Chinese attempts in the late 1950s to dissolve traditional families, villages, and religious practices and replace them with communes did not succeed.[6] Similar patterns in Nazi Germany were retained at a high pitch, but the regime was defeated before the stability of the system could be tested in non-war years. Generally, it appears that direct penetration cannot long be maintained under ordinary conditions.

On the other hand, society-wide mobilization may be greatly enhanced by intensified *indirect penetration,* insofar as this creates sub-units more committed to societal goals and ready to cooperate with the elites to this end. The indirect method features the state's influence over the *leaders* of the several sub-units. When leaders become convinced that the societal goals and the means by which the state proposes to gain them are sound, chances for activism rise, along with state responsiveness.

In discussing both specificity of control and penetration, we find important differences between the several modern totalitarian societies. While there is more direct penetration and prescriptive control in these societies, the degree is much less in the "mature" totalitarian countries, such as post-Stalinist Russia and other East European societies. In the latter, one finds a degree of pluralism and contextuating control. There are nation-wide collectivities with values, symbols, interests, and elites of their own which participate in the political processes. The military, the scientific establishment, and the industrial administration all possess some autonomy. Elites of groups deal with each other about joint policies. Still, the levels of specificity and penetration are relatively high.

A "Sensitizing" View of Societal Structure

The question of how the interests of the individual can reach elites so that they can "respond" to him is one of the most complex and crucial of all. What we will do is to give a "sensitizing" view of the structure and process, oversimplified in itself but implicitly referring to many of the other propositions we are developing.

The "mass society" theory, in its bare bones, maintains that elites manipulate the individual directly via demagoguery and the mass media (Hitler at Nuremburg rallies or on the radio, or "Big Brother" in Orwell's *1984*). The individual is atomized due to "loss of community"; the traditional solidary groups—family, church, guild—have lost their sway, replaced by the giant corporate bureaucracies of metropolis. Few individuals are active in politically-relevant organizations; therefore power is concentrated in state HQ which responds principally to a few power centers—the military and top offices of industrial, commercial, and banking companies: thus a "mass society," in which upward-moving consensus has no purchase.

Our view presents a different picture, one which increasing "activeness" may build upon to express consensus which will be translated into public policy. We hold that modern (and post-modern) society *retains forms of organization* which can represent the individual and that this representation can be multiplied by means of mobilization.

We see the individual as a member of micro-groups which form sub-collectivities along familial, neighborhood, ethnic, religious, and class lines. These are ecologically-based and possess a measure of solidarity through informal daily contacts and shared interests. The functions of these smaller units have changed, it is true: the family is more of a companionship unit, the church is less a spiritual community and more of a "social" one (through couples clubs, basketball teams, and other sodalities and fellowship ties). We see a society as being a "loose" mosaic of sub-collectivities, which in turn feed the politically active collectivities.

The individual is perhaps unaware of his membership in these groupings and their relevance to the political process, but when one or more organizations exist to mobilize and express the interests of its members, *the basis of representation and upward consensus formation is present.* The state and the power elites are forced to listen to them and be responsive to them. In modern society this responsiveness was not high. In the active society, greater mobilization tends toward a greater equalization of power, with the result that the responsiveness distributes access and resources to all, or most, of the members of the smaller groupings. Societal power then approximates political power, and the ultimate values of equality, freedom, and individual dignity move within reach. In this way guidance theory reveals options of a truly revolutionary kind.

NOTES

*Detailed references will be found in *The Active Society*, pp. 456–465.

1. For a discussion of "classical" sociological thought on the decline of community, see Robert A. Nisbet, *The Sociological Tradition* (New York: Basic Books, 1966). For a critique of "mass society theory," see Daniel Bell, *The End of Ideology* (New York: Free Press, 1960).

2. Talcott Parsons, "'Voting' and the Equilibrium of the American Political System," in Eugene Burdick and Arthur J. Brodbeck, *American Voting Behavior* (New York: Free Press, 1959), pp. 80–120.

3. Norman H. Nie, G. Bingham Powell, Jr., and Kenneth Prewitt, "Social Structure and Political Participation," *American Political Science Review*, Vol. 62 (1969), pp. 808–832.

4. William J. Goode, *World Revolution and Family Patterns* (New York: Free Press, 1963).

5. Amitai Etzioni and William R. Taber, "Scope, Pervasiveness and Tension Management in Complex Organizations," *Social Research*, Vol. 30 (1963), pp. 220–238.

6. James R. Townsend, *Political Participation in Communist China* (Berkeley: University of California Press, 1967), pp. 207–209, 216.

CHAPTER XV

The Mechanisms of Consensus*

To become active, a society must build consensus among its several groupings. Consensus is a congruence in the perspectives of two or more units.[1] (We avoid the term "agreement" because it suggests too much of a conscious, deliberate process.) The society's goals and the means chosen to seek them must be acceptable to the major active groupings. Consensus implies that national policies represent "the consent of the governed"—the interests of all the groups and collectivities of the society. This consensus is then expressed "upward" to influence decisions by elites. How this consensus is built is the topic of this chapter.

Generally, societies have a low consensus-building capacity, and a poor record to show. Democracies have recently endeavored to reallocate wealth, to alter the relations among races, and to integrate nations into larger communities—yet only minor changes have been accomplished. Master plans for the development of several backward countries came off the drawing boards in the 1950s; most of these have failed.[2] Even revolutionary regimes have fared poorly with societal guidance; Soviet attempts to abolish the state, religion, and stratification have not succeeded.[3] Proponents of one of the more promising communal forms—the Israeli kibbutz—are largely disillusioned.[4] *In each case, low capacity to build consensus contributed to the failure.*

Notes for this Chapter are on pages 180 and 181.

Cohesion, Flexibility, and Surprise

A country's social structure, of course, provides the background for its consensus-building. The fewer the cohesive societal bonds and links, the greater the load active consensus-building must carry. When state power is high, consensus-building tends to be postponed until after a new program is announced (thus inviting resentment). Common values, shared by members of associated but competing groups, strengthen the chances for consensus-building.

From the viewpoint of the student of consensus, individuals and groups are *not seen as fixed and given.* Rather, they are viewed as changeable. Otherwise, the hammering out of wide-ranging understandings would be impossible. Often, for example, a group's position on an issue is not fixed but vague and fluid, and is thus subject to movement toward some compromise. "Surprises" can occur. This is quite important, but often unrecognized, e.g., by "class" theorists. Or a group may decide to revise its position *instead of being left out* of the final "treaty" between previously antagonistic groups. Intergroup discussion may introduce new items and knowledge which encourage alterations. All in all, this kind of resilience of social actors and their groups means that consensus-building is available in a large variety of situations. This has often—though not always—been true in history, and is true today.

Normative and Utilitarian Bases

Some social scientists maintain that consensus is not a prerequisite of societal action. This may be true, but we believe that some degree of consensus is needed for *effective* action. We also assume that high dissensus has a cost—it alienates. Since we are interested in the conditions under which goals are realized, we wish to pinpoint the factors which *reduce* rather than increase this cost. Among the *bases that favor consensus-formation* are normative, utilitarian, and processual factors.

As to *normative* factors, there are shared values making some options unthinkable (e.g., bringing the number of death-penalty executions in the states back to pre-war levels), others legitimate, and still others desirable (e.g., reducing crime, poverty, addiction). Many groups will consider alternative actions *within the latter two* sectors.

Utilitarian bases for inducing consensus revolve around the fact that all societies constantly allocate a variety of assets. When a particular allocative pattern becomes taken for granted, it constitutes another foundation for consensus. Social security in the U.S. in the 1960s, for example, was widely accepted. Although its boundaries were contested, no group favored its abolition. In another example, the welfare state emerged from the recognition by affluent groupings that *some* reallocation of assets in favor of weaker members of society must be conceded if the consensus is to be maintained. President's Nixon's 1969 address favoring family assistance represented a further move in this direction. When such programs work well—provide a "pay-off"—consensus gains even more.

In addition to normative and utilitarian *bases* of consensus, ongoing *processes* of consensus-building can be utilized. The optimal relationships between these bases and the ongoing processes, we suggest, are roughly as follows: Ongoing processes use the consensual bases to define the issues and sharpen the debate by narrowing the range of alternatives considered. The specific consensus reached on "live" issues tends to fall *within the context set by these bases,* thus adding to it and reinforcing it. Most democratic or open systems contain margins for discussion of several value-backed alternatives.

It may not be necessary, always, to gain support before a new action occurs. A new activity that initially generates hostility or indifference but later wins the support of the relevant actors gives more promise than an activity that is initially supported but increasingly opposed during implementation. This should be considered as a hypothesis, to be tested in practical affairs. For example, the 1954 Supreme Court decision might have decreed that all public schools must desegregate the following September; some success with such rapid change had indeed occurred earlier.[5]

In short, consensus need not be present before an action, on all matters, or among all actors, but some consensus is a prerequisite for a high degree of realization of goals, in the long run. There cannot be an active society without a comparatively high *capacity to build consensus;* otherwise the increased activeness would entail a highly imposing and, hence, distorting form of tyranny.

Guidance Powers of the State

The major action agency of modern societies is the state —usually the national government. The state and its control and governing functions are an engine of societal mobilization. Before the society can guide itself toward widely shared goals, the state must move in that direction. The state commands enormous powers—legislation, taxation, enforcement agencies, and economic power. Further, it is via the state that consensus is most readily formulated, since the mechanisms for consensus-building are explicitly structured around it, as in political leadership, legislative bodies, political parties, and interest groups.[6] Unlike other units, it creates at least a minimal role for most members of the entire society—that of citizen; and it possesses —although it does not always use—coercive powers over groups and individuals.

The state does not merely carry out the wishes of member groupings; it has a power of its own and can exercise leadership. *Its power is great* under certain conditions: when lower groupings are weak (as Hitler decimated them in 1933), and/or when the officialdom have established themselves as a bloc (as in the Third Republic of France) or have been fused with a non-state organization (a party or the military) or a collectivity (e.g., the gentry in traditional China). The state, however, *has little autonomy* when it acts merely as referee among the several groupings or is under the control of a few of them and serves as their tool.

Even in the latter variation the state never merely reflects societal consensus; it always has an orientation and a power of its own. Through the tiers of the political process, societal power (coming up from the various collectivities) is converted into political power to guide. En route, some groupings gain and some lose, depending upon state decisions.

The relationship of societal power to consensus-formation is so close that the consensus reached reflects the distribution of societal power: who gets what, when, where, and how. A change in the distribution of assets among the various groupings of society (which is basically what we mean by social change) may originate in a sub-unit of the society, or with the state. But no matter where a change starts, it *must pass through the conversion process, by which ideas and demands are converted into political policy.* We now explore the various mechanisms for conversion and, hence, consensus-building.

Two Types of Consensus-Formation

The process of consensus-building typically falls between the two extremes of the "interwoven" and the "segregated" types. When segregated, it takes place in specialized structures like parties and legislatures which are distinct from population groupings. These "semi-process" the divergent perspectives of assorted collectivities, working as intermediaries between blocs and the society-state. A good example is the selection of the President of the U.S. The segregated type is typical of capitalist democracies.

Interwoven consensus-formation is carried out by the normal interaction among groupings. In folk societies these can be kinship units and tribal religious groups. In the more mature totalitarian societies, settlements are often reached through the guidance of one group—party or military—that penetrates the other units and limits their choice of options.

Segregated consensus-formation seems more effective than the interwoven kind, although it is unable to produce more than a low level of activeness. Hence the need for *combined* forms.

In a diversified modern society, consensus is formed more easily if a two-or-more-tier structure is used. On the first and lowest tier, the participant units (e.g., sub-collectivities) are combined into subgroups according to the relative affinity of their perspectives. Each of these subgroups forms consensus among its members. From each is sent a representative up to the next tier, which is composed only of representatives. Their number is smaller and their diversity of perspectives less, because they bring an "average" view of their constituency, not an extreme one. These representatives may then forge a consensus for the whole.

If the diversity is still too great, a third tier may form, composed of "representatives of the representatives." The averaging effect will be repeated, and consensus may result. Whereas the first level is made up of spokesmen for sub-collectivities, the higher levels are composed of political parties, the local governments, and national agencies. The final consensus is occasionally returned for ratification to the full membership (e.g., national elections). Usually, only a few alternatives—those that have been processed through the structure—are presented. When, however, the membership is presented with the full range of alternatives, the consensus-formation processes have failed. If the higher tiers favor one side against another, the results are also questionable, being less than consensual. All things considered, the larger the number and the greater the diversity of the perspectives of a group of units, the more difficult it is to achieve a consensus. This is one of the greatest challenges facing pluralistic societies.

Anglo-Saxon countries rely heavily on the lower levels, usually leaving only two alternatives for the last round. This round often focuses on "classical" issues: change as opposed to consolidation on domestic matters and militancy as opposed to moderation in foreign affairs.[7] Multi-party systems as in Italy, Holland, and Austria reserve more consensus-formation for the higher and more formal levels.[8] There is a weakness with both forms. In the bottom-heavy structures, too many alternatives never survive the lower tiers; too much processing—hence, elimination—takes place within the many "checks and balances" of the various sub-collectivities. The more top-heavy structure reinforces a passive electorate.

No group ever "gets its way" in this process, and some amount of alienation results as goals are bargained away. Yet *a more authentic alteration of the perspectives* of a given group can take place in the jockeying and deliberating processes. Thus the net amount of alienation is reduced while policy is created and the society moves off dead center. Crucial to our argument is the fact that groups can and do alter their positions; they can be induced to shift their perspectives.

INCREASING BOTH BASIC COMPONENTS

The quality of societal guidance is greatly affected by the quality of its two basic components—control (which moves downward) and consensus-building (upward)—and by the relative degree it uses one of these as opposed to the other.

In the control-consensus "mix," totalitarian societies emphasize control and democratic societies emphasize consensus-building. But in neither form has the active society emerged. *Totalitarian societies are overprescriptive,* deficient in their consensus-building, and therefore prone to alienation. Democratic societies are higher on consensus but low on control; they "drift."

The most effective "mix," we believe, is to *increase both components.* A democracy, to gain active guidance, must increase its control or political intensity, all the while maintaining its high consensus and expanding its bases by mobilizing the erstwhile excluded groups. Both control and consensus meanwhile must be made more authentic by using less coercion and persuasion and more education.

It is important here to note the counter-arguments to the popular assertion that control means regimentation. Simmel believed that freedom is not the absence of guidance but rather guidance that allows every man to be free.[9] Mannheim stressed that *freedom is to be planned.*[10] With respect to the use of property, more particularly, anthropologists agree that its use is subject to societal control in the interests of all members, even in the simplest tribes.[11] Drawing on these ideas, we believe that it is not more control that is needed, but rather a *qualitative change toward a more encompassing but not prescriptive control,* more closely related to consensus-building and less coercive and alienating. The correct balance is difficult to specify and may be reached *only via the political process.* It does appear, however, that the democracies, especially the U.S. and countries like Uruguay, tend to err in the opposite direction: they are underplanned and undercontrolled. They often permit the narrow freedom of a few to impose rigid constraints upon the freedom of the many. The freedom of advertisers, gun manufacturers, and pharmaceutical industries (to name only a few) is much more effectively protected than that of the public. "Natural" processes work far too gradually.

A classic case of confusion over government regulation occurred in 1905.[12] Senator Nelson Aldrich of Rhode Island, speaking against pending pure food laws, based his argument not on the interests of the food industry (which he championed) but on threats to the "liberty of the people." He asked if a man should be penalized for eating or drinking something proscribed by the government. The speciousness of his argument was exposed by Mark Sullivan: "The Pure Food bill put no regulation on any consumer; all its regulations were on makers and sellers. The only prohibitions in the bill were few: against selling diseased meat, or decomposed food, or dangerously adulterated food." *Far from limiting the consumer's freedom, Sullivan said, the law enlarged it.*

The history of the past 150 years has indeed shown that *the western democracies have moved to raise their levels of control while maintaining consensus.* Starting with various social welfare measures in Europe early in the 19th century and in the U.S. with the ICC of 1887 and the Sherman act, contextuating controls have risen. The same history demonstrates, however, that the change is slow and is resisted and delayed at many points. Policies not favored by powerful units are not implemented *until an internal crisis* (e.g., widespread rioting) *or an environmental one* (e.g., war or pollution) *reveal the overwhelming need for them.*

The resulting lag brings alienation and resentment at the rigidity of the society, and can be measured in cost terms. For example, some Swedes advocated a shift from driving on the left-hand side of the road to the right in 1945. At that time the change was expected to cost about 37 million kroners. By the actual time of change, 1967, the number of cars had increased enormously and the cost was estimated at 600 million. Totalitarian elites, for their part, tend to "overshoot," as in the cases of the Soviet NEP and the Chinese "Great Leap" of 1958. They fail to obtain both consensus before moving and realistic *knowledge* of the factors involved and hence produce frustration and alienation.

Three Paths to Change

Modern societies, of course, have engaged in some searching for effective means to reach their goals. We shall now explore these attempts. They can be divided into three broad types, *each of which seeks to link the segregated control units with the consensus-building units:* (1) the combination of societal knowledge-production and decision-making units with consensus-building units (toward interwoven planning), (2) change of ownership to bring control and consensus closer together, and (3) the rise of normative criteria which reduce the distance between control and consensus units.

How to gain more control and at the same time more consensus-building has concerned social planners for decades. This search becomes critical as men recognize the need for guidance and as new post-modern technologies appear. *Today, for the first time in history, developed nations may possess the capacity for the broad—but not overly specific—contextuating control that can bring guidance without tyranny.*

Planning before the post-modern period was remote, utopian, or overmanaging. The early "rationalistic" planner would produce a master design, perhaps attractive on paper but quite remote from both consensus building and from control.[13] It was segregated and apolitical, required a large application of power, would invite massive resistance and alienation—and was thus rejected.

INTERWOVEN PLANNING LINKS CONTROL AND CONSENSUS

"Interwoven" planners attempt to *integrate control, knowledge, and consensus-building units.* They discover first the perspectives of the decision-makers, then the perspectives of those likely to be affected. A still much higher level of articulation of planning and guidance comes when decision-making units and planning units are less segregated. This is the case with the European Economic Community, the French General Planning Commissariat, and the British National Economic Development Council, all post-modern agencies.[14]

These West European "interwoven" units engage in give-and-take with the elites of the collectivities which will implement the plans. The British NEDC, for instance, includes equal numbers of representatives of labor and business, working with public and governmental spokesmen. EEC committees out of Brussels comprise similar kinds of representatives, working with the several national delegations and going on location to the countries being planned for. In these consultations, *both the plan and the perspectives of the units are altered* to allow for more consensus and for less alienating and more effective control, thus increasing the chances for successful operation. The plan almost never assumes a capacity for *detailed forecasting or prescriptive control;* it aims only at keeping the guided processes within a context. One stated goal is to "civilize capitalism," getting rid of the buccaneers and chiselers.

Planning agencies differ greatly in the assets they hold for use in the political give-and-take. Segregated planning requires no such assets, since they are not empowered to give-and-take. Some "interwoven" units hold only normative power, appealing to the larger responsibilities of labor leaders, businessmen, and so on. Other planning agencies command utilitarian assets: tax concessions, low interest credits, subsidies, priorities in export or import licences, and so on.[15] Only rarely does planning use coercion; the very notion of consensus implies voluntary rather than forced cooperation.

So far, contextuating, interwoven planning has remained mostly in the economic area. A more active society will intervene in several areas: in education, the guidance of professional services, and in changes of status relations (desegregation, the absorption of new types of immigrants in Australia). Democracies have moved slowly toward these tasks. Britain moved earlier and more deeply into education than the U.S.[16] France acted quite deliberately with the Fourth Plan's goal of "a more complete view of man" rather than strictly economic planning.[17] The Scandinavian and Israeli planning of non-economic sectors is well-established, although there is little evaluation of effectiveness.[18] Other democracies (even West Germany) have accepted more planning in more areas than the U.S. But even here—where planning has been ideologically unpopular—the government has entered into tentative planning in the areas of race and model cities and has begun the control of population by supporting birth control programs.

Legislatures have been one of the foci of consensus-formation. Yet it is frequently noted that their power is declining, relative to the executive branch.[19] Executive agencies gain more *knowledge* than the legislature, and more experts are entering executive offices than legislative ones. This loss of power by legislatures is compounded by the fact that the units which their members represent are often *regional* while post-modern planning units are *functional or national.* The regional type was found in relatively "pure" form in feudal societies. The representative structure of the U.S. still has strong regional (often rural) bases, more so than that of Britain or Scandinavia. Where the regionality of a society is considerable, the tier of consensus-building below the political parties must become trans-regional and the relevant sub-units must be "functional"—for example, labor unions or intellectuals—and not regional.

"MIXES" IN PRIVATE AND PUBLIC SECTORS

Considerable political-economic controversy—to say the least—has raged over public vs. private ownership of property. Totalitarian societies rejected private ownership as non-consensual and adopted state control, while capitalistic societies did the reverse. In recent years, however, both types of societies have modified their extreme positions, one toward the acceptance of market mechanisms and the other toward more societal controls. It is popular to say that they are becoming more like each other. We suggest that both seem to be moving toward a third type—one in which no specific mode of societal guidance prevails but in which there are various combinations of ownership, management, and utility rights and benefits in the economic sector and also in health, education, welfare, and other activities.

Such "mixed" guidance societies entertain combinations of state and private enterprises (such as automobile manufacture in France), and privately owned as well as state-owned firms, co-ops, public authorities, regulatory agencies, and so on. The state typically maintains contextuating control (rather than the stricter prescriptive control) over wide areas. Such "mixing" appears to be not temporary, but a permanent feature of post-modern society. The key question is not whether state control will grow in the U.S. or private control in the Soviet, but *which combinations are likely to emerge* and what are the ways in which their relative efficacy, quantity, and quality of output, suitability to different sectors, responsiveness to the members' needs, and challenge to role performance can be determined.

Co-ops, for instance, link control and consensus more closely than most other units but are highly unresponsive to non-members and to general societal needs. Regulatory commissions which set the contexts without owning or managing are effective when two groups, such as labor and business, countervail each other, as with the NLRB. But where a commission deals with situations in which an organized industry faces unorganized consumers (FCC, ICC, CAB) it is less effective.[20] In still other areas, some public enterprises have affected the conduct of private ones, the impact of educational television upon commercial networks being a mild example. Finally, the threat of state intervention can lead to "house cleaning" or self-regulation, as with Hollywood in the 1920s.

Which "mix" is the best remains to be specified. Generally, a guidance system which relies heavily on inter-unit adjustment —whether among private firms or among co-ops—will neglect societal values and needs, such as the rights of weaker groupings. Prescriptive control from above, on the other hand, tends toward over-management and alienation. Hence we expect the societies that combine contextuating state control with the delegation of bit control to several groupings to be the most active.

THE IDEA OF "SOCIETAL USEFULNESS"

Recent years have seen the rise of a new and important criterion on which to base the conception of the relative investment in public as opposed to private pursuits. This is the notion of "societal usefulness," or "social responsibility." More and more, individuals and groups are expected to act less selfishly, to act more like the professional.

While skeptics assert that all organizations, be they public or private, act to promote their own interests, some shifts can be noted. The Committee for Economic Development, for example, published its new ideology of public responsibility in the late 1940s.[21] Profit maximization by firms was questioned as the single purpose of business enterprise. Rather, obligation of the firm to customers, suppliers, employers, and the general public was recommended. This movement followed the growing trend for bigger and bigger corporations and was paralleled in the newspaper industry, which was characterized by fewer newspapers with larger circulations. Many corporate giants, and of course most entrepreneurs, have not warmly embraced these altruistic ideas.[22]

The changing prestige accorded to the various occupations is also relevant. In 1966 a sample of college seniors, asked which career they favored, *ranked business far down the list.*[23] The professions were given 55 per cent of the choices; teaching, 24 per cent; business and government, 9 per cent each. Similar findings have been reported elsewhere. Teaching has become more popular with young males, and the role of the intellectual has likewise risen in esteem. The Peace Corps, VISTA, and "poverty" work became popular. Thus notions of "culture heroes" are shifting from entrepreneurs to the more service-oriented roles.

Greater interest in activities dealing with symbols (e.g., cultural and political activities) rather than with material objects is a corollary development to the rise in the emphasis on societal usefulness. Consensus-building is facilitated because while material scarcity is inevitable, there is no limit to participation in cultural and political life. The combined rise in both affluence and education in the U.S. has contributed to this shift. (On this basis Western Europe and the Soviet Union may be entering an age of conspicuous consumption at the same time the U.S. is outgrowing it—but they may later follow suit.)

The mechanisms of consensus, when operative and effective, assure that the power elites will endorse the agreed-upon programs. This means that those who have little or no active voice in the councils of consensus also affect policy and action, if only by their disaffection or passive resistance. And their needs command the same ethical status as those of the more powerful. The concepts of responsiveness and equality—to which we next turn our attention—serve to extend this line of analysis so that it embraces these groups which consensus tends to exclude.

NOTES

*Detailed references will be found in *The Active Society*, pp. 495–502.

1. For a review of definitions and approaches, see Theodore M.

Newcomb, "The Study of Consensus," in Merton, Broom and Cottrell (eds.), *Sociology Today* (New York: Basic Books), pp. 277–292.

2. Albert Waterston, *Development Planning: Lessons of Experience* (Baltimore: Johns Hopkins University Press, 1965).

3. Barrington Moore, Jr., *Soviet Politics* (New York: Harper & Row, 1965).

4. Richard D. Schwartz, "Democracy and Collectivism in the Kibbutz," *Social Problems,* Vol. 5 (1957), pp. 137–147.

5. Kenneth B. Clark, "Desegregation: An Appraisal of the Evidence," *Journal of Social Issues,* Vol. 9 (1953), pp. 2–68.

6. Robert A. Dahl, *Modern Political Analysis* (Englewood Cliffs: Prentice-Hall, 1963), pp. 1–13.

7. Amitai Etzioni, "Consensus Formation in Heterogeneous Systems," in Etzioni, *Studies in Social Change* (New York: Holt, Rinehart and Winston, 1966), pp. 136–151.

8. Maurice Duverger, *Political Parties* (London: Methuen, 1955).

9. Kurt H. Wolff, *The Sociology of Georg Simmel* (New York: Free Press, 1950), p. 122.

10. Karl Mannheim, *Freedom, Power, and Democratic Planning* (New York: Oxford University Press, 1950), pp. 29–31, 111–112.

11. E. Adamson Hoebel, *Anthropology* (New York: McGraw-Hill, 1966), p. 414.

12. L. L. L. Golden in *Saturday Review,* April 13, 1968, p. 93.

13. Robert Boguslaw, *The New Utopians* (Englewood Cliffs: Prentice-Hall, 1965), Chapter 3; Waterston, *Development Planning, op. cit.,* pp. 263–268, 333–339.

14. Neil W. Chamberlain, *Private and Public Planning* (New York: McGraw-Hill, 1965); John and Anne-Marie Hackett, *Economic Planning in France* (Cambridge: Harvard University Press, 1963). For a recent U.S. case, see John Fischer, "The Easy Chair," *Harper's,* Oct. and Nov., 1968.

15. Everett E. Hagen and Stephanie F. T. White, *Great Britain, Quiet Revolution in Planning* (Syracuse: Syracuse University Press, 1966), p. 102 and footnote 2.

16. Martin Trow, "A Question of Size and Shape," *Universities Quarterly* (G.B.), Vol. 18 (1964), pp. 136–137.

17. Andrew Shonfield, *Modern Capitalism: The Changing Balance of Public and Private Power* (New York: Oxford University Press, 1965), p. 227.

18. Benjamin Akzin and Yehezkel Dror, *Israel: High Pressure Planning* (Syracuse: Syracuse University Press, 1966).

19. John P. Mackintosh, *The British Cabinet* (London: Stevens, 1962); James A. Robinson, *Congress and Foreign Policy-Making* (Homewood, Ill.: Dorsey, 1962).

20. Marver H. Bernstein, *Regulating Business by Independent Commission* (Princeton: Princeton University Press, 1955).

21. Francis X. Sutton *et al., The American Business Creed* (Cambridge: Harvard University Press, 1956).

22. John Kenneth Galbraith, *The New Industrial State* (New York: Signet, 1968), Chaps. 10, 11, 15.

23. *Newsweek* (reporting a poll by Louis Harris), May 2, 1966, p. 85.

CHAPTER XVI

Transforming Unresponsive Societies*

We have stressed the relevance of consensus-formation because elites in the active society need to be aware of the interests of all of its members. But awareness is not enough. Consensus may still result in policies that favor coalitions of the powerful. Such an excluding consensus will perpetuate alienation in the weaker units. To be fully active, the society must also be *responsive* to the needs of all its members. In this chapter we explore the concept of responsiveness and its relation to the concept of political *flexibility*. We then discuss conditions under which responsiveness is limited, and finally the conditions under which sources of unresponsiveness may be overcome. We shall note the importance of changes in the *distribution of power*, as political mobilization brings new groups into public participation.

The rise of new groups to political consciousness has signalled the growing democracy in western societies. The high degree of exclusion of many groups in the 18th and 19th centuries (workers, the middle class, ethnic minorities) declined only gradually. Further "broadening of the base" continues in post-modern society. *The active society will be markedly egalitarian:* groups are increasingly mobilized to expand their political power.

Notes for this Chapter are on page 194.

Flexibility

The concept of *flexibility* denotes the capacity of a society to transform itself. *The most flexible systems are willing to alter their "political shell" to admit mobilizing groups into places of power.* Less flexible systems resist longer before they "open up." If they continue to be exclusive, the frustrated resentment and alienation of the rising groups may pile up and "erupt." Britain, for instance, is considered more flexible than France and Italy; these are more flexible than Spain. The Russian revolution brought a sudden and violent end to the considerable inflexibility of the czars.

When political flexibility is high, societal power and political power coincide. The state's distribution of rewards and facilities no longer allots great slices of the pie to traditional elites. Few rigidities prevent continuing *reallocation of resources* as new groups enter the arena. "Rotten boroughs" in British history and the over-representation of rural areas, and of business and military interests, in the U.S. are well-known examples of rigidity. *Over-organization* presents as many problems as the sociologists' favorite bugaboo—social disorganization. At the level of the individual person, elites in active societies will be persons of great tolerance for change.

REVOLUTIONS AND BIT REFORMS

Revolutions are commonly depicted as direct changes in societies, especially in class relations. As we see it, revolutions often are initially changes in members' *access* to control of the state; after a revolution, the state more accurately represents the relative power of groups. The new groups now introduce societal changes, including those which neither these collectivities nor the state had been able to bring about. *The more peaceful avenue of transformation* requires a more flexible reallocation of power, granting more to the rising groups, and curtailing the power of groups no longer able to marshal consensus in their own behalf.

We are *not* referring to the familiar dichotomy between revolution and reform. Small reforms may furnish momentum to a revolutionary thrust, or they may appease and deflect it. Reforms alone are no assurance of a close and continuous "fit" between society and state. The demarcation line is thus not between revolutions and reforms but between revolutions and transforming reforms on the one hand and bit reforms on the other. Nor do we accept the opposition between violent revolutions and peaceful reforms. Some revolutions ("ripe" ones) are quite peaceful (e.g., the Nasserite one in 1952), while some reforms follow or bring considerable violence (Mao's "cultural revolution" of 1966–1968). Numerous riots, "palace revolutions," and coups are not revolutionary.

DEMOCRACY AND FLEXIBILITY

While political flexibility is occasionally high in a non-democracy and low in a democracy, we suggest that on the average, political democracy is the least rigid existing form of government. What is most essential in democracy is not merely the holding of elections, but *the institutionalized change of the party in office* following and in line with changes in the societal power of the several collectivities. *Elections reflect the degree of success of inter-election consensus-building.* Democracies also are less rigid because of the way they articulate knowledge and power. Non-democracies rely on upward communication links such as intelligence networks, which tend to bias their reports about the changing power of sub-groupings.[1] The representative structure of democracy provides the only political organization in which there is an institutionalized combination of upward communication *and* power.

Yet a democratic government, however flexible, may not be responsive. The main differences between a highly flexible polity and one that is also responsive are (1) in the ratio of members included in political processes as opposed to those who are excluded, (2) in the degree to which *political power is equally distributed* among the members, and (3) in the degree to which *societal power (and assets) is equally distributed* among the members. How to extend the political base?

The Ideal of Near-Equality

Societal consensus is worked out among actors that differ in power. Even when consensus is high, decisions favor the strong more than the weak. The strong can hardly be expected to give up their power, although they may grant concessions when normative values favor benefits to the weak.

The question of whether or not complete equality is feasible or desirable is a highly abstract one. Perhaps the real question confronting theories of social guidance is the specification of the conditions under which *gross inequality* can be substantially reduced. It may be that *substantial equality* of the main distributive assets is the most a society is able to sustain without violating other values (e.g., achievement orientation). Thus even a high quality of consensus will result in some alienation, because the weaker sides will not gain their will. And the less egalitarian the power distribution, the more the collectivities that will be alienated.

One central difference between democratic (especially capitalistic) societies and active societies is that the former stress consensus but are inegalitarian; they include many passive and alienated groupings. *Democratic societies are much less responsive than they are flexible.* Active societies emphasize an egalitarian distribution of power; they contain few passive or alienated groups and are responsive. *Two sources of unresponsiveness of societal elites* can be specified: deficiencies within the elite control centers themselves, and maldistributions of societal power within the society.

DEFICIENCIES IN CONTROL CENTERS

Throughout Chapters 4 to 10 we discussed failings in the

control centers. Major deficiencies (to give a brief review) include: insufficient knowledge, in the form of poor collection, analysis and synthesis of information; a focus on bits rather than on more encompassing contexts; and the stubborn retention of obsolescent perspectives—all leading to poor reality-testing. Instrumental factors include shortage of assets and decision-making that is either overly incremental or rationalistic. Among the insidious expressive factors are the ideological dogmatism of elites and their staffs that prevent them from realistically assessing incoming messages about changes in the needs and powers of the member units and about the effects of signals issued earlier by the centers. Finally, there are communication snags that distort incoming and outgoing messages, and such "cultural" problems as differential access and understanding between elites and rising groups such as workers, minorities, and students.

Means for reducing these sources of unresponsiveness have also been discussed, in Chapters 9 and 10 on decision-making and also in our discussion of the role of "fundamental criticism" in checking elite actions and aiding in their reality-testing. These measures increase the effectiveness of control and permit elites to be more responsive.

A second barrier to responsiveness has also been introduced, starting with Chapter 11. This is power, especially the *distribution of power that may exert strong pressure on elites to maintain policies favorable to the powerful—and thus continue their unresponsiveness to the remainder of society.* This oft-told tale fills history books.

TWO DIMENSIONS OF POWER DISTRIBUTION

Two dimensions of power distribution—not one—affect responsiveness: the distribution of power among the member collectivities and that between them and the state.

So far as the members are concerned, *the more egalitarian the distribution of power among them, the more responsive the overlayer will tend to be to their needs.* The "giants" will, not surprisingly, dominate decisions as to "who gets what." The rest, excluded from power, will show high alienation. On the second dimension, a "medium" amount of overlayer power will make it more responsive than either a low or a high degree. As we have said repeatedly, a weak government will allow the society to drift; a super-powerful one will overmanage and impose policies running counter to the members' needs.

These two dimensions of power distribution—among collectivities, and between them and the state—define the main types of power structures which make for unresponsive guidance mechanisms. A brief historical review will illustrate the types.

EXAMPLES OF UNRESPONSIVENESS

In early capitalist societies, the controlling overlayer is weak, and much societal control falls into the hands of industrial and commercial groups. The Haymarket affair symbolizes this period for the U.S. More recently, "modern" capitalism witnessed some rise in the power of the working classes; the power of the state increases, but capitalists retain much influence. Welfare capitalism is a post-modern extension of this form, as in the U.S. The power of both the state and non-capitalist classes rises, but *without a basic change in structure.* We move toward the optimum responsive society in countries which for long periods were under the rule of Social Democratic parties, as in Scandinavia. Here state power approximates the "medium" level, and the relative power among groups is fairly egalitarian. A continued rise in egalitarianism without an extreme increase in state power would lead to the active society, thus to optimal responsiveness.

Turning now to societies with a strong state and weak members, we find those usually described as "totalitarian." Even here, differences in responsiveness can be found. Nazi Germany and post-revolutionary Russia and China demonstrate high state power but a considerable "crunch" on the autonomy of member groups. The Soviet Union currently seems to be moving in the responsive direction, by reducing the power of the Party-State and awarding more influence to various members (labor, management, intellectuals). The same is true of several of the East European Socialist Republics, Yugoslavia being the first to break away from rigidity and to accept considerable autonomy in local units.

The movement from totalitarianism to greater responsiveness will require more than relaxing the vigilance of police and granting the expression of human and civil rights. To reach the active society such a nation needs to grant these rights but also to bolster its consensus-formation and shift from prescriptive to contextuating control, without curtailing overmuch its degree of state power.

Power and Rising Groups

Power is distributed unequally but is never monopolized by one grouping.[2] The central question for the study of transformation toward the active society is not the degree of concentration, but whether or not the aggregation of power by some members is *sufficiently great to prevent the accumulation of power by rising collectivities.*

The historical evidence on this point is by no means clear. On the one hand, capitalistic societies such as Britain have moved in the "active" direction. In the U.S., the rise of the welfare state and the ability to mobilize first a labor movement and then a civil rights movement suggest that a transformation may be possible.

On the other hand, a generation of efforts in the U.S. to redistribute the wealth in less inegalitarian form has yielded little change. The "share" received by the top 5 per cent of incomes decreased between 1929 and 1944, but has declined little since then.[3] The European social democracies have done somewhat better. As to the concentration of economic control, the 200 largest American corporations controlled nearly half the corporate wealth in 1929.[4] A generation later, despite new laws, a decline in the legitimation of big business, and some government efforts, the concentration had not significantly decreased.[5] Hence, radicals may still claim that any changes were merely expedient tokenism.

A counter-argument can be marshalled: *Western societies did transform gradually at least once,* and transformation is underway again. The change in Britain and the U.S. from agricultural to industrial societies entailed the transformation of all the major institutions of these societies, especially the shift of political control from the aristocracy and rural collectivities to capitalist, urban centers. The second transformation, now in progress, involves an expanding welfare state, government guidance of the economy and other societal processes (e.g., education), and the mobilization of weaker collectivities. Thus the argument cannot as yet be settled, but it seems clear to us that the ability to advance the transformation of democracies by mobilization of the underprivileged collectivities *has not been exhausted.* Whether the active society will arrive—this remains to be seen.

The traditional argument has centered around the transition to state socialism; nationalization of the means of production was taken as the measure of progress. More broadly, state regulation is considered essential for transformation. We hold, in contrast, that the active society could be achieved with quite modest nationalization and indeed might be blocked by a high degree of state regulation. The economy of an active society might well be "mixed" between private, public, and cooperative sectors. Several changes are crucial: some expansion of state power and the participation of all member collectivities; much reduction of private regulation; and a big increase in public, cooperative, and various "mixed" forms of regulation. A society that seems tolerant of only a small move toward state socialism might also become an active society, whereas a society embracing state socialism may not encourage the kind of activation that the move toward the active society needs.

Some writers assume that there must be a showdown, which is won by either the "socialist" or the "capitalist" forces. We feel, however, that it may not be a matter of "revolution or reform," but of various degrees of the use of force. Barrington Moore has completed a monumental study along these lines, and has shown that all the cases of industrialization he studied involved revolutions from above, "the work of a ruthless minority." [6] While each case witnessed violence, the level of violence differed significantly, and so did the societal resistance to change. China is at the "revolutionary" end; Britain and the U.S. are at the "violent" but gradualist transforming end; France, India, and Japan lie in between. The period of transition, in short, need not involve holocaust.

UPGRADING AND STATE ACTION

Clearly, the mobilization of weaker groupings is crucial in this analysis. To advance the transformation, the society itself, as well as the weaker groupings, must be mobilized. Why is this so? Does not society, which reflects the typically oligarchic power distribution, neutralize even the newly-won power of rising groups? This process is common, but to the extent that the *whole society "upgrades" itself—by adding to the societal assets—transformation is still feasible.* This comes about either because the total societal "pie" is enlarged via economic growth, or by more assets being allocated to non-private use. The GNP of the U.S., for example, is expected to almost double by 1975, as compared to 1965.[7] The total pie expands, so that more is available to the public sector.

We do not expect that mobilization in itself, either of the weaker collectivities or of the total society, will be sufficient to bring about transformation. Too many inequities in power will remain. The gains in power resulting from mobilization need to be *converted* into an increased share of the political control of the state so that assets can be reallocated in favor of the new groupings. Mobilization, that is, must bring structural changes, and inter-group re-shuffling must be complemented by reallocation legitimated by the state.

This need to "anchor" the gains of mobilization through state action to recognize the new power base has not always been understood by the mobilizers themselves. The anarchists' belief—that once the traditional power elites are weakened the oppressed will rise and never again be dominated—played a major role in the failure of the 1905 revolution in Russia. Before mobilization truly guarantees greater equality, laws and other institutional arrangements must formally acknowledge the new, less oligarchic, rules of the game.

Where the Mobilizers Come From

We have recommended that mobilization of currently weak collectivities, and of society in general, is a key to the transformation of societies. But we must also answer the question: Where do the mobilizers come from?

The target groups—the weak collectivities—are easy to identify and describe. Their members possess a low level of societal consciousness; they tend to accept the prevailing view of society and share in its consumption obsession, mass culture, and political apathy. We also assume that alienation among them is high and that their situation is inauthentic (ideas which we will discuss in the next three chapters).

Ongoing forces in post-modern society somehow seem to be preparing them for mobilization. This is especially true with the rise in education levels—even granting that much of the "education" may be specialized "training" for specific jobs and may deflect them from broader horizons of consciousness. Still, the semi-educated are more reachable than the uneducated, and better jobs may produce the familiar "revolution of rising expectations" which, if frustrated, produces resentment with the system.

In addition, the potential base of active mobilizers seems to be broadening. Mobilizers are recruited largely from two strata, each yielding a potential trickle of organizers. First, there are those who deal in symbols, especially professionals, college faculties, students (often those whose parents were liberal, critical, and permissive),[8] and other intellect workers. The second most important recruitment source is the unbalanced collectivities, especially those whose economic status is higher than their prestige ranking. The growth of the first group is a product of the knowledge revolution and has been recognized as "real" in at least one study;[9] the second stems from economic mobility.

ORGANIZATIONS OF MOBILIZERS

Next come the *organizations* of the mobilizers, which tend to be core-organizations of service-collectivities, seeing service to others and to a societal cause as a central value. These groups (the British CND—Committee for Nuclear Defence—and the American SDS and SNCC) *resemble early religious orders* in several ways: personal and organizational austerity; funds used for purposes of collective action; a high percentage of one's time collectivized and mobilized; the members' special clothing and hairstyle marking the vows of poverty and distinguishing members from non-members; a combination of tight organization with informality and anarchy; much wandering from place to place; no formal and little informal social distance between leaders and followers; suspicion of and from the outside world. These norms produce a very high conversion ratio; the sacrifice of personal gain allows a small group to act with great efficiency.

Transforming movements rise out of a combination of service-collectivities and one (or more) underprivileged collectivities with high mobilization potential. But not all attempts at building transforming movements are successful. For a group to act as mobilizer it has to (1) be educated enough to create counter-symbols and ideologies; (2) be sufficiently alienated to be fundamentally critical; (3) command enough organizational skills to serve as part of the controlling overlayer of the transforming movement; (4) accumulate sufficient knowledge to evolve an appropriate theory of society and political strategy; and (5) be able to prevent personal, apolitical deflections. Student groups often meet these conditions; groups in bohemia, the professions, clergy, and "unbalanced" ethnic minorities in the middle class tend to meet them less fully. Coalitions of such groups have successfully energized many movements, from the suffragettes to Castro's revolution.

Limitations on mobilization include the subjugating forces of the society and the low action capability of the target collectivities. There are also deficiencies in the "control" prowess of the mobilizers such as those listed above, especially in societal knowledge and analysis. A stark example is the case of the early anarchists, who renounced all organization of the bureaucratic types.[10] More recently anarchists have adopted organizational strategies and gained more success, as in the French syndicalist movement.

Similarly, a weakness of the old and new left radical mobilizers in post-modern U.S. is their deficient societal analysis and political strategy. They tended to romanticize ideologically the weakest collectivities and to limit their activation attempts to them. The Communist Party's concentration on working with Negro-Americans in the 1930s and 1940s is a case in point.[11] This tactic is to be contrasted with one which seeks to expand the mobilizers' base and then to work with semimobilized groups and potential allies.

A final barrier is inherent in the very expansion of the functions of the post-modern state. The state employs greater numbers of professionals and university personnel, with the resulting co-optation or "taming" of these potential mobilizers.

We have examined in considerable detail the structure of post-modern society in the effort to discern sources of unresponsiveness to the "have-nots." Relations between groups and their relative power have been found to be crucial in determining which of them can mobilize to participate effectively in consensus-formation and thus to influence the decisions of overlayers in the vital question of who gets what. With greater equality of power between groups, the state is placed in the position of guiding the society toward achievement of goals, not merely for traditionally powerful groups but for all. Hence our continuing interest in the *change* of social structures and social relations over time. One further point remains. We have suggested that society is inauthentic, that social relations are without firm foundation, that elaborate facades conceal underlying realities producing alienation. The final three chapters will deal with this issue.

NOTES

*Detailed references will be found in *The Active Society,* pp. 541–548.

1. Giles Perrault, *The Secret of D-Day* (Boston: Little, Brown, 1965), pp. 166–167. German officers provided Hitler with information to suit his preconceptions, including his misconceptions.

2. For a different view see C. Wright Mills, *The Power Elite* (New York: Oxford University Press, 1959), esp. pp. 274–278.

3. Ida C. Merriam, "Welfare and its Measurement," in Eleanor B. Sheldon and Wilbert E. Moore, *Indicators of Social Change* (New York: Russell Sage, 1968), p. 744.

4. Adolph A. Berle, Jr. and Gardiner C. Means, *The Modern Corporation and Private Property* (New York: Macmillan, 1933).

5. Robert J. Larner, "Ownership and Control in the 200 Largest Nonfinancial Corporations, 1929 and 1963," *American Economic Review,* Vol. 56 (1966), pp. 777–787.

6. Barrington Moore, Jr., *Social Origins of Dictatorship and Democracy* (Boston: Beacon Press, 1967).

7. *A "Freedom Budget" for all Americans: A Summary* (New York: A. Phillip Randolph Institute, 1967).

8. Kenneth Keniston, *Young Radicals* (New York: Harcourt, Brace & World, 1968), Chap. 2.

9. *Ibid.,* pp. 135–140.

10. James Joll, *The Anarchists* (Boston: Little, Brown, 1965), pp. 108–110.

11. Nathan Glazer, *The Social Basis of American Communism* (New York: Harcourt, Brace & World, 1961), pp. 169–180.

PART V

FROM ALIENATING TO ACTIVE SOCIETY

CHAPTER XVII

The Authentic Society and Basic Human Needs*

Post-modern society "inherited" an alienating structure. This is seen today in industrialization and bureaucratization and a worship of "rational," instrumental, impersonal materialism. To these often alienating features, post-modern society has added an increased capacity for *manipulation,* producing a *sense* of responsiveness where none actually exists. Of course there have always been men who were unaware of the basic facts of their socio-political lives and, thus, acted in opposition to their interests and their private selves. It is the *scope and depth* of such false awareness and commitment that seem to be new. We will proceed to examine two consequences of this structure—alienation and inauthenticity—in relation to "basic human needs."

The relative significance of manipulation becomes more evident with a decline in the importance of non-symbolic, material bases of alienation. *Modern society with its enormous success in production can feed, clothe, and house most of its members.* Inequality stems from a *psychology* of scarcity, rather than being strictly economic. Thus *symbolic* distortions, and their resolution, are key topics in post-modern activation.

Alienation as Resentment

The concept *alienation* has been defined in many ways.[1] As we use it, it has one core: the unresponsiveness of the

Notes for this Chapter are on page 206.

world to the person, which subjects him to forces he neither comprehends nor directs. *Early industrial society and its dark satanic mills epitomize alienating society.* Market relations and administrative structures, which were developed ostensibly for the greater happiness of the greatest number, in effect produced a warped society, one that stood between its members and the satisfaction of their basic needs.

Alienation is not only a subjective feeling of resentment but also an expression of the objective conditions which expose a person to forces beyond his understanding and control. Alienation has both institutional bases and individual psychic consequences. As these two conditions are often confused, we refer to the society as *alienating* and to its members as being *alienated.* Thus the roots of alienation are not in interpersonal relations and intrapsychic processes but in the societal and political structure. *This structure is what the active society will seek to transform.*

CONSEQUENCES OF ALIENATION FOR THE EXCLUDERS

Alienation is encompassing, embracing the whole society or the whole individual. That a worker is dissatisfied with his work is not sufficient evidence that he is alienated, and one who is satisfied with his work may still be alienated. When alienation exists, it encompasses most, if not all, social relations. And the concept does not assume that the individual need be aware of his alienation.

Moreover, alienation affects both the excluded groups and those who do the excluding. The excluded obviously are affected; the society is unresponsive to them and to their needs. The excluding groups are also affected; the process of exclusion creates a distorted social world which they cannot escape. Highly alienating structures rely heavily on coercion and manipulation; this brutalizes and dehumanizes the rulers as well as the ruled, as studies of concentration camps, totalitarian structures, and police forces demonstrate. Again, the market system of modern society places a high value on material objects and material values; the incapacity of the participants for uninhibited and holistic affection for human beings, themselves included, *diminishes the humanity of all members and not just the workers.*

An alienated man may be passive or active. A passively alienated man is subject to societal forces and apathetically acquiesces to his condition. An actively alienated man is also subject to such forces, but he recognizes a commitment to change the stifling institutions around him. Personal activation within alienating structures is always distorted and incomplete, as there cannot be personal realization without societal activation. We shall see, however, that personal activation can contribute to societal transformation toward an active society.

Inauthenticity as False Appearance

The concept of alienation has lost some of its analytic power because it has been applied to diverse phenomena. We suggest here, therefore, a sub-category of alienation which we refer to as *inauthenticity*. A relationship, institution, or society is *inauthentic if it provides the appearance of responsiveness while the underlying condition is alienating.* Objectively, both alienating and inauthentic structures are *excluding,* but inauthentic structures devote a higher ratio of their efforts than do alienating ones to concealing their contours and to building the appearance of responsiveness. It is this trait that underlies much of the criticism of the mass media, Hollywood, public relations, and the advertising characterized by the opprobrious term "Madison Avenue." Subjectively, to be alienated is to experience a sense of not belonging, and to feel that one's efforts are without meaning. To be involved inauthentically is to feel cheated and manipulated.* The alienated feel that they have no power; the

* A statement by a college student: "If I wear a beard and a girl I love stays in my room all night and I sleep with her, I'm a beatnik and in a state of moral decline. If I shave and

inauthentic feel that they have pulled a disconnected lever, without knowing where and how, so that shadows are confused with reality. The alienated are imprisoned; the inauthentic work a Sisyphean labor. The individual counterpart of inauthenticity is *hypocrisy*.

Authenticity exists where responsiveness exists and is experienced as such. The world responds to the person's efforts. It is the fate of the inauthentic man that what he knows does not fit what he feels, and what he affects is not what he knows or is committed to. His world has come apart; it is "phoney." *The alienated man*, by comparison, is likely to be excluded to a greater extent from all three sources of activation (consciousness, commitment, and power-holding), laboring in someone else's vineyard, factory, laboratory, or army. He is characterized by despair, resentment, disaffection.

BASES OF INAUTHENTICITY

When both the appearances and the conditions are nonresponsive, we have outright alienation. When both are responsive, we have an authentic relationship. Inauthenticity exists when appearance is responsive but *reality is not*. (The fourth category is rare—conditions allow for participation, but the situation goes unrecognized and not acted upon by the participants; the "latent" situation will be short-lived because genuine participation is bound to be noticed.) With authentic relationships, the person's orientation is active; those caught in inauthentic or alienating relationships are active to the extent that they seek to transform their condition.

The term inauthenticity has been used by *existentialist* writers in two ways.[2] First, in the narrow usage as "false consciousness," mostly applied to the working classes; in fact, all relationships, not only consciousness, may be affected, and all

go to a whorehouse, buy stocks on the South African exchange that net me a large profit, and sign up for the CIA when I graduate from college, my behavior is unquestioned and my integrity assumed." Quoted by Robert Coles in *The New Republic*, Vol. 154 (May 28, 1966), p. 21.

groups and even society itself may be inauthentic. These writers refer to the condition of being disconnected and of foregoing one's responsibilities, whereas we use the concept in the absolute sense that *authenticity is not possible under alienating conditions.* While the actively alienated man may play a significant role in transforming his condition and in creating the opportunity for authenticity, as long as this transformation is not advanced, he is not free from the effects of his alienating condition.

Existentialists have also used the concept for a highly voluntaristic theory, stressing the personal responsibility of the actor in a society largely predetermined by supranatural or economic-technological forces. This is a paradox, and bespeaks a basically negative view of society we do not share. We see the person as less free, though he has options which ethics may command him to exercise, toward the greater sum of his freedoms. We view society, however, as less determined, as *open to restructuring by the efforts of the members.*

Limits to Manipulation

The concepts of alienation and inauthenticity make the assumption that men possess certain *basic human needs.* Nobody has ever *demonstrated* the existence of any form of human needs; many "lists" were drawn up earlier in the century, but each was rejected by most other psychologists. Yet psychologists and sociologists still, very tentatively, talk about such needs.

Why do we argue the existence of basic needs? Alienation and inauthenticity refer to a lack of responsiveness, *but unless we assume that those to whom the social structure does not respond have needs which are independent of the needs produced by their relationship to the structure, the idea of unresponsiveness is inconceivable.* There can, of course, be some lack of coordination between a society's child-raising system and its productive and allocative structure, or some time-lag in the accommodation of personalities to changing societies; these factors could account for some unresponsiveness. But it could, in principle, be eliminated as readily by changing socialization as by changing the productive and allocative relations. Thus, *without an analytic concept of autonomous needs, it must be concluded that there is, in principle, no limit to manipulability*—that man's needs are infinitely pliable in that they can be changed to fit the societal structure, rather than require a transformation of the structure to achieve a higher level of responsiveness. In the earlier situation, man is a puppet; in the active society, man can be free.

Parsonian and Meadian Approaches

Two of the most widely prevailing theories of social action today—the Parsonian and the Meadian[3]—differ from both the Marxist and the Weberian perspectives; the former assume, in effect, that human needs are almost completely pliable within broad physiological limits, such as the need for heat, sleep, and food. Social needs—e.g., for affection—are recognized by these theories, but they stress that such needs may be satisfied by many institutional arrangements. This means that (1) most of the variance in socio-cultural patterns must be accounted for by properties other than those of the basic needs, (2) differences in the *psychological costs* of various patterns must be accounted for by properties other than those of the basic needs, and (3) there is no analytic place in these theories for an unresponsive social structure, although in fact man gets trapped in one just the same.

Among the things society must do, two are relevant in this existing theory: it must provide one or more "outlets" for the basic needs of its members, and it must socialize members to accept those outlets. Some members, of course, are not successfully socialized; they may be resocialized (e.g., in a rehabilitation institution), or "socially controlled" by police, courts, and jails. Further, although the possibility of broader malfunctioning followed by greater deviance and pressure for reform is recognized, it is assumed, in principle, that there are few if any limits to socialization and social control. The best indication of this assumption is the presence in these theories of conceptions of deviant individuals, sub-cultures and even social movements, but rarely of a *deviant society*.[4] The notion of a deviant society, however, is the key concept for the alienation tradition—a society whose structure is contrary to "human nature" and disallows the satisfaction of basic human needs. If these are to be satisfied, it is *society* that will have to be restructured, and fundamentally.

We suggest a "moderate" version of this approach to personality-society relations. We prefer this version to the one prevailing in sociology because we reject earlier approaches which saw human needs as demanding one specific or narrow set of outlets or which viewed socio-cultural patterns as reflecting "basic personality."[5] Before suggesting the limitations which basic needs impose on the structure of a responsive society, let us indicate the needs we consider basic.

Basic Human Needs

No originality or completeness is claimed for this list of needs. It is tentative, ignores physiological drives, and is meant to be provocative. What we seek to illustrate are the opportunities to test empirically the key proposition that *the flexibility of basic human needs is limited, and they can be more readily and fully satisfied in some societal structures than in others.* Some structures are less responsive and more alienating than others, and there are significant limits to the manipulability of the members.

We suggest that two things humans need are *affection,* or love, cohesion, or solidarity; and *recognition,* or self-esteem, achievement, approval. While recognition is granted for judged quality of role performance and tends to be specific and universalistic, affection resides in expressive relationships and is holistic and particularistic. Recognition is less scarce than affection, in that any one person can grant recognition to more people than those for whom he can have affection.

A third basic need is for *context,* variously referred to as the need for meaning, orientation, consistency, synthesis, or "wholeness." Each person plays many roles in many groupings, and these shift with aging and with changing times; he "needs" some embracing frame of reference or context to organize for himself his diverse perceptions, emotions, and beliefs. A disjointed self pulls itself apart; it needs this kind of "harmonization," gestalt, or "identity."

These three relatively specific needs supply to the individual the basic inputs of purpose, security, and meaning. *Three other conditions* facilitate the achievement of the basic needs. There is the need for repeated gratification; whatever the source of gratification, large lapses of time between instances of it are frustrating. More frequent rewards (compliments, signs of affection, reinforcements to one's context) are quite welcome. Further, it is rewarding to be able to *anticipate* that gratifications will continue regardless of changing events, that there is some expectable stability of gratifications due to the social structure and one's role in it. Without such stability anxiety rises, and the person is more open to stress from within and manipulation from without. The anxious man, for instance, who seeks security by repressing his individuality will suffer from deficient recognition. Finally, there is the requirement of variance in a social structure. Each individual is to some extent unique in his personality and interests. Thus a satisfying society will provide a pluralism of social roles and norms as outlets for a wide assortment of personalities. Alienation is higher, the greater the gap between the range of unique personalities and of roles for them to fill. Not everyone could be, or would want to be, a physician, an executive, a movie star, or a patrolman. A society, for example, whose production system demands many more highly skilled men than the I.Q. distribution can provide is likely to be alienating.

To repeat, these three basic human needs and the three conditions *have not been demonstrated as fact.* Other scholars have asserted, and will continue to assert, a different set. Our purpose is to make a provisional test of our "need" hypothesis *by showing the high cost of maintaining a society which frustrates these needs.*

BASIC NEEDS AND SOCIAL STRUCTURE

We suggest: *the more a social structure allows for the satisfaction of the basic needs of its members, the less the structure will be alienating.* Participation by the members comes to assure the responsiveness of the structure to their basic needs. Ultimately, there is no way for a social structure to discover and adapt to the members' needs without the participation of the members in shaping and reshaping the structure. *Participation becomes a major social invention and instrument.* Complete satisfaction of the needs, of course, is impossible; the gratification of some needs reduces the ability to gratify others because of the limitations of scarcity—as in the sometimes difficult choices in conferring affection and recognition in interpersonal relations. If all the available societal energy were invested in gratification, assets would be consumed but not replenished, and anticipatory action—"executive" planning for the offenses and defenses of the future—would be neglected. Human social life entails frustration, as Freud stressed, but at all levels, from the intrapsychic and interpersonal to the societal and cultural.[6] Individual sublimation involved in the deferment of gratification is never completely successful, and there always remains an element of suppression and a residue of conflict.

Thus there is no social life without some alienation. It is the degree and distribution of this alienation that require our attention. If some is inevitable, the amount can be reduced. We conclude that most alienation (above and beyond the irreducible kind) *is the result of a specific societal and cultural pattern and can be decreased by changing that pattern.* While persons can be socialized into roles which provide low, infrequent, and uncoordinated gratification, the costs of such arrangements are high, which, as we shall show, provides the empirical test of the existence of underlying, but frustrated, basic needs.

NOTES

*Detailed references will be found in *The Active Society,* pp. 655–657.

1. Melvin Seeman, "On the Meaning of Alienation," *American Sociological Review,* Vol. 24 (1959), pp. 783–791.

2. Martin Heidegger, *Being and Time* (London: S.C.M. Press, 1962); Jean-Paul Sartre, *Being and Nothingness* (New York: Washington Square Press, 1966).

3. Talcott Parsons, *The Social System* (Glencoe: The Free Press, 1951), Chapter 6; George Herbert Mead, *Mind, Self and Society* (Chicago: University of Chicago Press, 1934).

4. Parsons, *op. cit.,* Chapter 7.

5. Our position is close to that of Alex Inkeles, *What Is Sociology?* (Englewood Cliffs: Prentice-Hall, 1964), pp. 49–61.

6. Warren Breed, "Suicide and Loss in Social Interaction," in Edwin S. Shneidman, *Essays in Self-Destruction* (New York: Science House, 1967), pp. 188–202.

CHAPTER XVIII

The Human Costs of Inauthentic Society*

We have argued that man has certain basic human needs, and we have indicated what we think they are, as well, or poorly, as they can be known. Now we must show that these needs are not infinitely changeable but really "are" basic to man. Then we must ask *what social structures come closest to meeting them.*

Some of the fundamental components of this social structure have already been suggested: the responsiveness of elites to society, their flexibility in admitting rising groups to a share of political power, and authenticity in the society. In spotlighting structures and processes that would *weaken* the active society, we will examine the extent to which "deviant behavior" results from the "costs" of a distorted social structure.

The Pervasiveness of Basic Human Needs

How to verify the validity of the concept of basic human needs? One should focus on comparisons of the socialization and social control "costs" of various roles, groupings, and total structures, and on the visible indications of frustration or strain. *The fact that a man can be made to carry out almost any role is not proof of his flexibility, so long as the personal and social costs of the efforts are not counted.* We suggest (1) that there are differences in socialization and social control costs and the levels of frustration of any two roles; and, above all, (2) that

Notes for this Chapter are on pages 219 and 220.

the costs are higher when the roles are less "natural"—i.e., allow for less satisfaction of the basic human needs. Anthropology has shown that men may be socialized to be warlike or peace-loving, passive or hyperactive, monogamous or polygamous: man is pliable. But some structures stunt gratification more than others by ignoring the basic needs. This "cost" question is typically ignored in the literature.

The same point can be made about human "persuadability." Can an adult's character be changed? is a frequently asked question. Some generalizations seem warranted. Most studies of efforts to affect "deep" personality variables—psychoanalysis, psychological experiments, and "brainwashing"—show these efforts to have little and infrequent effects.[1] "Brainwashing," the most intensive and encompassing of these, affects only a minority of its subjects, and this minority includes people predisposed to such effects and/or to the view they were "persuaded" to accept. Moreover, many of those positively affected remain so only so long as they stay in the affecting environment. Some "converts" may continue their new behavior if they remain relatively isolated with the other zealots. It is mainly when *the total environment is changed and persists that a deep effect continues,* as when adults emigrate or when Communist governments established themselves in Eastern Europe. These costs are obviously very high, but to change man, institutions must usually be changed first. Recent work with encounter groups may open up new ways to lasting personality change, but most men develop a sense of congruity about self and others that resists dramatic change.

The great amount of literature about *attitude changes,* which are less deep than personality changes, suggests that under most conditions, only "bit" changes, rather than contextual changes, are attained. Thus, adults can be influenced to shift from one brand of soap to another, but the ability of the mass media to change our attitudes about religious, ethnic, or political matters is limited.[2] Its influence is most frequently a matter of *reinforcement of existing attitudes, not conversion.* And most important, the *great cost of successful persuasion*

is not taken into account. Highly unusual social conditions must be constructed (e.g., isolation imprisonment), and a high level of frustration must be inflicted. Hence if the concept of cost is added, we reach the opposite conclusion: not that man is "persuadable," but that under most conditions he is not. Personality strives for unity, consistency. There is something tenacious about man's clinging to familiar people and to accustomed, shared lifeways, ways that seem "natural" to him and which we feel (but have not demonstrated) are expressive of his basic human needs.

For all these reasons the society has no alternative but to guide its own transformation if it would liberate its people and seek its goals.

Measuring the Frequency of Alienation

How may we measure the personal and social costs of a social structure? This is no simple task, due to several knotty methodological circumstances.

One school of thought maintains that contemporary man is not alienated at all. For instance, attitude surveys reveal that from 75 to 90 per cent of workers interviewed say that they are "reasonably satisfied" with their jobs.[3] Others point to the high standard of living, the seeming "happiness" of many people at work and in their homes, the weak support given to radical movements, and the like. Some critics, tongue in cheek, say the people enjoy their mass society, consumption gluttony, and suburbia. They conclude that the whole notion of alienation is a verbal invention by intellectuals, that it scarcely exists.

At the other extreme, alienation is said to pervade modern society. The average man is called a boob, a sucker, "hollow" in the lonely crowd, the victim of economic and political elites, property relations, mass culture, and an estranging bureaucracy.[4] Or, these spokesmen argue, the symptoms of alienation are buried so deep that they cannot be tapped and measured by social science methods but can only be sensed by empathy.

We take an intermediate position. We recognize the need to show empirically that modern social structures do produce the personal and social costs of alienation. Yet it may be that these costs may register *only when those social science methods are applied which probe the deeper layers of personality.* Existing "depth" methods have shown the existence of alienation in individual attitudes, revealing caverns of despair, resentment, hopelessness, and so on.[5] These projective and other "stress" methods can be improved: indeed, this is a major task for social science. But there is evidence that high personal costs are found when we look where we can expect to find them—*below the surface* of life in an inauthentic society.

Differences in the social cost of one form of life rather than another can be shown rather easily. Systems which allow for no personal achievement (thus the basic need for recognition) are so costly they are unsustainable, such as *austere* communist states, kibbutzim, and other utopian settlements. Generally, austerity tends to erode in the direction of more frequent and higher levels of gratification—e.g., the transformation of communal settlements. Other "unnatural" systems can be sustained but only with much policing (i.e., with high social control costs) or for very select groups (religious orders) so that the socialization costs are tolerable. Stretched society-wide, they would perish.

RELATING ALIENATION TO SOCIETAL DISTORTIONS

To support the basic proposition, it is not enough for depth methods to show that people exhibit severe anxieties and frustrations in post-modern society, and for comparative studies of social costs to show that industrial societies invest a good deal in manipulation, diversion, and police activities. It is also necessary to show *that these costs are accountable to the structural distortions of society.* It is insufficient to report high rates of crime, psychosis, suicide, alcoholism, drug addiction, and child neglect, since it is occasionally argued that they were "always" high.[6] We must show they have risen with the rise of modernization. Most sociologists assume such a rise although the data do not justify this belief.

Most of all, the crucial question is the specification of *the ways in which* unresponsive roles, institutions and societal structures increase these personal costs. And *the ways in which* a climb in the responsiveness in the roles and structures decreases alienation in a previously warped society.

It may be futile to search for a one-to-one relationship between one symptom and the unresponsiveness of one structure to one basic human need. The theory of alienation, or of deviant behavior, does not provide such specific links. Ten persons, facing the same alienating structure, may *respond* in ten different ways, according to their past and present circumstances and the traces on their personalities. Yet careful longitudinal case studies with representative samples may highlight such personal dynamics in response to such alienating processes. *We do not have good enough studies of this kind.*

Our evidence, to date, on the causal links is not satisfactory. This is due to several circumstances of current social science: the above-mentioned polarization of survey-methodology and empathy, the weakness in studies of the etiology of deviance and its relation to social structure, and the relative neglect of the notion of basic human needs. Still, the association between modernization and increased personal costs has been a major theme in literature and social study for 150 years, and the available evidence for the association is at least stronger than that opposing it. There is evidence that forms of authentic activation (as in collective projects, and certain types of group therapy) reduce the incidence of such symptoms as drug addiction, alcoholism, delinquency, and the culture of poverty.[7]

A Modest Test: Suicide, Needs, and Social Structure

We will now advance this discussion one notch, by relating "distorting social structure" to the basic human needs, using one form of deviant behavior—suicide—as the focus.

Studies of suicide (both of rates and of individual cases) arrive at several generalizations, the pertinent ones for our test being that there are higher rates among males than females; more during periods of economic slump (especially among businessmen); more in advanced than in folk societies; and above all, many suicides among males who have failed at job or business by being fired, unemployed, refused promotion, and the like.[8]

These are all the data we need. What is their relation to basic human needs and to social structure? Here a theory is required; many sociologists would use some form of "anomie" theory or self-other theory, and we will draw from both of these.[9] We will plead our case using a single aspect of social structure, that of role, or more particularly role expectation. Every society prescribes certain tasks for persons in various positions, and allots rewards for the proper performance of these tasks, so as to motivate the person to accomplish the needed function.[10] What, now, is expected of the adult male in urban society? Basically, he is expected to be working at a job and to be doing well in it—earning promotions and raises in pay. *This becomes the one key criterion of man's worth in society;* it fixes his income and his prestige, both. It is the biggest factor in his success or failure. Now we can link this structural factor to the non-satisfaction of the basic needs. The job-role-failing man certainly is not receiving recognition from those around him (he is not "a successful man" and "doesn't deserve" recognition). This same failure, we expect, also costs him heavily with his needs for affection and identity.

We see this emphasis on work-achievement—a prominent cog in the social structure—as an over-confining box for millions of men. To suggest a much broader vision, the fact is that all men play many roles; to single out the one role of work as the definitive measure of his worth is to overplay drastically the need for *achievement* in the "economic" role. A more authentic society would "label" a man's contribution in several roles. Man's breadth of interests and modes of expression—we assume

—are unlimited; there are thousands of ways of expressing himself in the pursuit of gaining satisfaction of the basic human needs. The man who kills himself out of shame over his work-failure may be "good at" dozens of roles. For example: his role as father, husband, or brother; friend of X or friend of Y; neighbor, citizen, Scout leader, storyteller, church member, fisherman. In the successful playing of any of these roles a man could win —given a broadening of the criteria of success in life—much (1) affection, (2) recognition, and (3) context. Under this more human and responsive structure, frustration and suicide would recede.

Focusing on society's authenticity permits us to take a good look at *the standards society uses to reward (and therefore to control) individuals.* Society does need to reward those who do things important to the society. Sparta prized its soldiers; the U.S. for about a century lionized its business tycoons. Attention must still be paid, however, to those whose personalities fail to meet these heroic expectations. More pluralistic standards—more options for modes of playing roles—is one way to reduce the alienation. The role of commercial tiger fails to meet the basic needs of many men; what it did meet was the demands of a society based upon the Puritan ethic and the devil take the hindmost. At first glance the suicide resulting from work failure could be seen as flushing out the man not needed in the social system. Study of the victims reveals, however, that these men were not in fact the worst failures; they *felt* themselves to be failures, but really they were men who had accepted in exaggerated fashion the Puritan "success" ethic. Moreover, for every work-failure suicide, there must be hundreds of men "alive" whose needs for affection, recognition, and context are poorly met by current social arrangements.

Our case of suicide and work is only one example of such arrangements, but it embodies the anomie principle: society demands things from the individual but fails to provide him with the means to carry them out.[11] In each instance the basic human needs are ignored and alienation—and in its wake all kinds of deviant behavior—mounts.

The Industrial System forced all its eggs into the single basket of efficient work achievement. *Post-modern society cannot afford this luxury.* Work, like leisure should be rewarding in itself.

Many societies have distributed these rewards for successful role performance more judiciously. In doing so, they are implementing a wider band of values or options than the narrow "achievement" values of success in marketplace and payroll. We cannot, it is granted, prove these societies to be more responsive than ours, but they do appear more authentic and less alienating. A shift in this direction could, of course, retard the standard of living, but this is not certain, given advances in cybernetics and technology.

Finally, if our suggestion seems extreme, it echoes the message coming from countless young people in their noisy criticism of contemporary values and social structure. They have watched their fathers climbing the hierarchy of middle-class organization man, and they don't like what they see. Some of the fathers murmur their own reservations about the system. Those who have known "work-role failure" suicides can place the blame for the death upon the distorting, role-rigid society.

The argument can be turned around: How many "successful" business and professional men harbor no resentment against the system and show no symptoms of pathology, from alcoholism to neurosis to vague feelings of non-fulfillment of the basic human needs?

We have not yet spoken of female suicide. Here the data show numerous cases in which the woman has had enormous difficulty—especially for women in their 20s and 30s—in marriage and in motherhood.[12] The same general principle applies to women: role failure. The modern woman is expected to succeed at the roles of wife and mother. Those who fail, or who would prefer a number of other roles—perhaps job, career, or just "friend"—are subject to the same lack of satisfaction of basic human needs. A social structure rigid and imbalanced in its role demands takes its toll here as well.

We have used the example of suicide because of our own research in that field. What of other forms of deviance related to distorting or rigid social structures? The same kind of "role failure" problems also appear to be present somewhat in cases of mental illness and drug addiction, and possibly alcoholism.[13] Moving even further, juvenile delinquency has been seen as a consequence of exclusion from rewards as felt by lower-class boys.[14] And certainly prejudice and discrimination directed against out-groups have structural bases. Broadly, a basic source of deviance is injustice—a pattern firmly rooted in the distributional function of social structure. That injustice can promote alienation is clear. The inauthenticity that erects curtains of haze between reality and perception, we feel, encourages doubt, uncertainty, and dropping-out that could be minimized in a more straightforward system. A society in which people feel they must engage in instrumental orientation and conspicuous consumption, and which leaves them with unnecessary status frustration, cannot be termed authentic.

Increasingly Authentic Standards

It also may be that *more authentic standards* have been introduced into post-modern society *under the impact of humanitarian values,* with the result that costs in the form of symptoms merely "seem" to be higher, but are in fact not so. Racial and ethnic prejudice is the best example: three decades ago few persons saw prejudice and discrimination as a major social problem, whereas today most people do. Objectively, however, more minority individuals are in fact treated better today than before, while discrimination "seems" much worse.[15] We see things today with more humanitarian—and therefore authentic—eyes. The same could be argued for physical and mental illness, aging, child-raising, alcoholism, poverty, and so on. This line of argument may weaken our central thrust of the need for guidance. On the other hand, we suggest that *in certain sectors western society has already blazed some trails of responsiveness.*

Individual Awareness of Inauthenticity

Because the inauthentic condition appears to pervade post-modern society, but has not received the attention given to "alienation," let us return for a closer examination of its persistence and its effects upon the individual. When a person is unaware of the inauthenticity of his condition, he is likely to feel listless, uncommitted, apathetic—unsatisfied in a global way. While this disaffection may focus on particular issues, *if those issues are corrected it shifts to others.* He cannot articulate the cause of his malaise because he accepts the facades around him as valid.

When mobilization removes, at least in part, the disguise which conceals the underlying reality, inauthenticity need not disappear. This is because disguises are reintroduced, so that continued effort is required to eliminate them, and especially because the disguises themselves are part of the societal structure which resists change. These "images" cloak the differences between the ideal and the real, which are sporadically referred to by critics but become lost again in endless diversions by institutional leaders and the mass media—hence again the needed function of continued fundamental criticism.

The *alienated* man who is actively conscious of his situation senses that he is excluded, whereas *the man who is aware of his inauthentic condition* feels manipulated and indeed is made to bless his captors. The alienated man sees before him a tall, unyielding wall. The man caught in an inauthentic situation feels entangled in a cobweb. *He cannot locate the source of his malaise to fight against it.* There is more guilt, because he senses that he shares in his own manipulation by allowing gestures and quasi-solutions to substitute for real change. The alienated man may sense that reality has been distorted and that he mirrors the distortion. The inauthentic man will in addition feel cheated, detached from reality, and will question his ability to grasp it; a smoke screen hovers between himself and his world.

Both the alienating and the inauthentic contexts tend to be impersonal. But the alienating context provides, especially for the actively alienated, a clear enemy as target. In the inauthentic context, more effort is expended in concealment and facades; while the members have greater vision because of the rising level of education and income, less can be glimpsed through the haze.

It is stressed that the person's acceptance, rejection, calculation, or even ambivalence in regard to a particular societal structure does not allow us to judge whether or not his commitment is inauthentic. A person who rejects the application of force to humans and is moved by genuine warmth and affection, who wheels-and-deals in the market-place and is ambivalent when faced with a mixture of these elements, might well be relating authentically to each of them. It is he, however, who loves the hand that beats him (as in concentration camps) and is calculative in his love relations (as in promiscuous liaisons) who is inauthentically committed.

The depth of the inauthenticity varies. It may be slight—some lip-service paid to a conflicting set of norms, like the free thinker in the U.S. claiming to be religious. Again, it may run deep, as for the homosexual who pretends to be a heterosexual, maintains a marriage, and accepts internally the norm of heterosexuality but realizes he cannot conform to it, or, the person who engages in "bit" criticism when it is really the systemic context that he consciously disapproves—an orientation shared by many liberals in the Soviet Union and the U.S.

The Dangers of Over-Commitment

Even though we have stressed that widespread participation is a key requirement for an active, responsive society, a discounting note must be sounded. Democratic politics cannot function, oddly enough, if all members are committed intensely on all issues. If all the citizens were fully mobilized and committed, consensus-formation, which requires a willingness to compromise, would not be possible. Commitment requires being active in some spheres *and being mobilizable when the contexts of the other spheres are violated.* Any democracy requires a "floating vote." The highly committed are unlikely to "float" and to allow procedure to take priority over the alternative they favor, *and* they feel intense about most issues. Thus intense and encompassing commitment tends to be associated with "extreme" political conduct and extra-institutional action.

The limitation of commitment, however, must have a special structure before it aids democracy: it must be low in regard to specifics but high as to contexts. Thus, democratic commitment is low to any party but high to the democratic process; i.e., democracy cannot be based on *encompassing* apathy. When few participate, oligarchies continue their rule. Similarly, there are basic values other than democracy that, when violated, bring the "contextually" committed out of their *partial* (or contextuated) apathy. Thus, the moderate who cannot become enraged about the violation of any value (e.g., various forms of pollution) weakens democratic politics as much as those who are extremely committed on most issues.

Ironically, another danger to superficially smooth politics is a recent "over-commitment" of intellectuals to "the politics of conviction." [16] These people support the war on poverty and condemn colonial wars not out of personal gain but because they believe their policies to be correct. Their commitment to justice and equality prevents these "true believers" from compromising for expedience; they are "difficult to deal with." In contrast, the older politics—"the New Deal system"—compartmentalized policy decisions: farmers made farm policy, unions made labor policy, defense contractors shaped procurement priorities, and so on. The old system "worked" with little conflict but also with little long-range goal-achievement. The new form promises much ideological conflict and much stout resistance from traditional groups. "The problem is that too many people are no longer willing to mind their own business." [17] In our terms, greater demands are placed on consensus-building.

Affective Relationships in Modern Society

Without diffuse, affective relationships, man cannot gain his basic needs of affection, recognition, and context. The human being is a *social* being. Affective relationships endure in micro-cohesive units such as the family and friendship groups. In turn, *these relationships need to be built into more encompassing units* such as the village or community, so that the person may extend his loyalties to the macro-units which set the contexts within which he strives to meet his basic human needs—both the cultural or symbolic context and the social or distributive context. The "flower children" of 1965-1967 heralded an ethic of love, but without basic re-structuring of the surrounding society the appeal was bound to fail. Modernization, during recent decades, is said to have created anomie by its undermining of *both* micro- and macro-cohesive units. We have already seen that this does not necessarily follow—that the old cohesive units have adapted and that new ones (e.g., employees' groups, church clubs, suburban "kaffee-klatching") have been created.

Many modern primary groups, however, have been called inauthentic. Modernization is alienating in that men more readily treat each other as instruments, rather than as persons valuable in themselves. *Inauthenticity enters when people pretend to be goal-oriented while actually they are instrumental,* when they pretend to seek friendship while actually they seek personal gain. The quasi-friendship of the salesman, the advertiser, or the status seeker does this, turning a latent function into a manifest one.

NOTES

*Detailed references will be found in *The Active Society,* pp. 657–661.

1. On psychotherapy, see Kenneth M. Colby, "Psychotherapeutic Processes," *Annual Review of Psychology,* Vol. 15 (1964), pp. 347–370; on brainwashing, see Edgar H. Schein, *Coercive Persuasion* (New York: Norton, 1961); and on psychological experiments, see William J. McGuire,

"Attitudes and Opinions," *Annual Review of Psychology,* Vol. 17 (1966), pp. 475–514.

2. Bernard Berelson and Gary A. Steiner, *Human Behavior* (New York: Harcourt, Brace and World, 1964), pp. 557–584.

3. Robert Blauner, *Alienation and Freedom* (Chicago: University of Chicago Press, 1964).

4. Paul Goodman, *Growing Up Absurd* (New York: Random House, 1956).

5. Edgar Z. Friedenberg, *Coming of Age in America* (New York: Random House, 1965).

6. Herbert Goldhamer and Andrew W. Marshall, *Psychosis and Civilization* (New York: Free Press, 1953).

7. For the effect of civil rights activity on drug use among Negroes, see *The Autobiography of Malcolm X* (New York: Grove Press, 1965); and Kenneth B. Clark, *Dark Ghetto* (New York: Harper & Row, 1965), p. 216.

8. Andrew F. Henry and James F. Short, Jr., *Suicide and Homicide* (Glencoe: The Free Press, 1954); Jack P. Gibbs and Walter T. Martin, *Status Integration and Suicide* (Eugene: University of Oregon Press, 1964); Warren Breed, "Occupational Mobility and Suicide Among White Males," *American Sociological Review,* Vol. 28 (April, 1963), pp. 179–188.

9. See Albert K. Cohen, *Deviance and Control* (Englewood Cliffs: Prentice-Hall, 1966), Chaps. 7–10.

10. Kingsley Davis and Wilbert E. Moore, "Some Principles of Stratification," *American Sociological Review,* Vol. 10 (April, 1945), pp. 242–249. This is "the functional theory of stratification."

11. This is Merton's "social structure and anomie" theory in Robert K. Merton, *Social Theory and Social Structure* (New York: Free Press, 1957), Chap. 4.

12. Warren Breed, "Suicide and Loss in Social Interaction," in Edwin S. Shneidman (ed.), *Essays in Self-Destruction* (New York: Science House, 1967).

13. Jerome K. Myers and Bertram H. Roberts, *Family and Class Dynamics in Mental Illness* (New York: Wiley, 1959); Seymour Fiddle, *Portraits from a Shooting Gallery* (New York: Harper & Row, 1967).

14. Albert K. Cohen, *Delinquent Boys* (Glencoe: The Free Press, 1955); and Gerald Marwell, "Adolescent Powerlessness and Delinquent Behavior," *Social Problems,* Vol. 14 (Summer, 1966), pp. 35–47.

15. John P. Roche, *Quest for the Dream* (New York: Macmillan, 1963).

16. Edward V. Schneier, "Intellectuals and the New Politics," *Bulletin of the Atomic Scientists,* Vol. 24 (October 1968), pp. 15–18.

17. *Ibid.,* p. 18.

CHAPTER XIX

Inauthenticity, Alienation, and Avenues to the Active Society*

The major flaws in post-modern society are continuing alienation and growing inauthenticity. We will illustrate the extent to which this is true by examining several areas: politics, work relations, childhood socialization, and mass culture. We will close by suggesting that projects, on several levels, show the greatest promise for curbing these conditions and for leading to the active society.

Inauthenticity in Political Institutions

In the history of modern democracies, *the period of alienation* saw large segments of society left out, disenfranchised. Later, the scope of exclusion was gradually reduced, but major segments (working class, various minorities) were still left unrepresented. These societies began to develop *elements of inauthenticity*—as well as alienation—when in the name of democracy, excluded groups were given the legal right to vote but by various devices the alternatives offered them still expressed the interests of elites. "New" groupings could not express their newly won power; *new societal power did not convert into effective political power.* The emerging group, therefore, despite token enfranchisement, eventually turns to "direct action" (from strikes to riots). Within these groupings a sense of cynicism develops, a distrust of politics and politicians. "You have to hold your nose to vote," said the anti-imperialists in the 1900 election, after their candidate misled them.[1] This is only one

Notes for this Chapter are on pages 235 and 236.

step from not voting, and two steps from rejecting the political system and its legitimacy.

Early labor parties, enamored of their newly won role in parliamentary politics, neglected the economic needs of the workers who voted for them. Soon they showed the familiar signs of inauthentic political mobilization—dissatisfaction, factionalism, secessions, and direct action. Examples are the German Social Democrats' efforts to avoid offending the Kaiser in 1912 and the MacDonald involvement in "parliamentary games" in Westminster.

Similarly, the post-modern period's increased reliance on mass media and manipulative techniques to "sell" candidates on the basis of their appearances (the "image") is successful: Members of groupings whose basic needs are not represented by these candidates still vote for them. Studies suggest, however, a fairly widespread sense of being cheated or of not being fully involved in the political process.[2] This seems to increase when the candidate stresses one theme, only to carry out the opposite policy once elected, as Wilson did in 1916, and Johnson did in 1964. Both campaigned as peace candidates and engaged in wars. The result is a generalized bewilderment.

A more extensive restudy of Western democracy from this viewpoint is necessary. A major reason for this system's considerable stability and continuity is that it was not always *unresponsive* to the newly emerging groups. When the left, anti-monopolistic groups prior to 1894 saw the U.S. so unresponsive that their commitment to the system was weakened, the Democratic party responded to them and, for a while, under the pressure of the Populists, represented the anti-business alternative. On the other side of the spectrum, as the conservatives became increasingly dispossessed, the candidacy of Senator Goldwater gave them an expression lacking since Herbert Hoover. Before 1964, they had felt increasingly cheated by the democratic process. The fact that there was little increase in non-democratic, right-wing direct action after 1964 suggests that most of the conservatives saw *the system* (though not the outcome), as basically fair. Thus, the conditions under which, and to what degree, the American polity is or is not responsive are still unsettled questions.

THE GAP BETWEEN SOCIETAL AND POLITICAL POWER

One major consequence of inauthentic democratic politics —and an almost endemic danger in post-modern societies—is that *new societal power is not converted into political power.* Or, emerging groups are forced into dramatic confrontations to gain the attention of elites. The condition leads to overdue and inadequate responses, direct action, the disaffection of intellectuals and, when extensive, to a violent transformation of society. One thinks of the U.S. urban riots of the late 1960s, France in 1968, and dozens of "modernizing" revolutions in other countries.[3]

It is generally agreed that the textbook model of democracy, in which the needs of the people "percolate" upward and provide directives for societal action, is unrealistic. Most of the flow in fact seems to be downward; various elites initiate and specify policy alternatives and gain endorsement by mobilizing the support of lower-echelon leaders. This more critical downward model presents a fairly accurate picture of inauthentic democratic politics and inauthentic consensus-building; however, *it omits the costs* (personal and social frustrations, and the like) when it claims to be a model of a well-functioning democratic system rather than a distorted one. Also, inauthentic politics cannot mobilize sufficient energy for higher levels of societal activation. At best they can *contain* the existing conflicts, but, as the differences among the various strata are not narrowed when consensus-formation is inauthentic, societal passivity is pervasive.

Passivity, it may be argued, is functional for those who benefit from the status quo. We would argue, however, that elites and "have" groups do not always seek to stabilize the status quo. Faced with rising social demands, *the more far-sighted elites do try to adapt,* even if they lose part of their assets in order to salvage the rest. For example, the British aristocracy and later the British bourgeoisie showed that they understood this point, at least better than their French brethren. But such adaptation must possess the organizational capability to bring the new groupings into genuine political participation.

RESPONSIVENESS THROUGH CONSENSUS

Authentic consensus-building, on the other hand, can *strengthen the responsiveness of elites.* It may "specify" the needs of members in such a way that differences among them will be reduced, thus increasing the responsiveness to *all* the members, despite their divergent positions. Members' needs, after all, can be served in a variety of ways (as hunger can be assuaged by different foods), and some concessions can be made by both sides without a sense of alienation from the game. This is the reason we suggest that a significant part of politics is not reallocative (with bloc A getting more than bloc B), but *re-educative.*

There is a difference between inauthentic politics and compromise politics. The latter is part of the authentic democratic process. The essence of responsive consensus-formation is that those who differ in their perspectives work out a "concurred" policy. This policy will not satisfy completely the original demands; the process entails some sacrifice of initial positions.

Shifts in Work Relations

As early as Sir Thomas More's day and continuing almost to the present, the unresponsiveness of commercial and industrial organizations to the needs of workers and of the society has produced widespread alienation. By comparison, work in the highly industrialized societies is less depriving and more remunerative but not more involving. Its organization is still basically non-participatory, and a good deal of the increased participation by the workers is inauthentic, as we shall illustrate below. At the same time, the distorting effects of work relations on other societal sectors have not greatly declined, though they have become less manifest. Inauthenticity is also generated in other sectors, such as the market and education, and is carried over from these into work relations. Thus we expect that *neither nationalization nor other forms of public ownership will remove unresponsiveness,* as is illustrated by oligarchic unions, exploitive cooperatives, and, of course, factories in socialist states.

Early industrial management-worker relations were dominated by open exploitation and alienation. *The introduction of "human relations"* (by the Mayo school and others) as a manipulative technique *marks the rise of inauthenticity.*[4] Worker participation in decision-making made few inroads in the basic power or asset structure and no genuine sharing of goals, and it has often had the deliberate purpose of draining energy from conflict politics, especially unionization. Yet "shared goals" are proclaimed.

In the realm of *labor organization,* open alienation prevailed in the period in which the right of workers to organize was denied. Early inauthenticity is marked by the organization of company unions actually run by management. Many unions, which originally provided genuine upward representation, gradually, by co-optation and other devices, came to act like company unions and are highly inauthentic.[5]

Studies show that American workers prefer high-paying alienating jobs to lower-paying, less alienating work. But this *does not prove that these workers favor alienating work.* They choose it to obtain the means to satisfy the consumption cravings and status anxieties that are rooted in their inauthentic off-the-job relations.

The preference for a culturally and politically active life over the pursuit of consumption, one could argue, is merely an intellectual's utopian dream. Hence it should be stated that *these changes have already started;* though they presently encompass only a few, the number of adherents is growing and acceleration can be expected. Second, we hold that a society will move in an active direction as more of its members discover and choose an authentic life; i.e., we expect that more people will live like intellectuals. Recall the discussion in Chapter 7; by the 1970s intellectuals had become one of the biggest occupational groups in the U.S. population. That other people will not have the opportunity to join them means that the society will not be fully active; but it will be moving in that direction. That inauthentic work and consumption have serious consequences for large segments of the population is a proposition that can be empirically tested; it rests on the indication of restlessness and a sense of being cheated.

John Kenneth Galbraith has illustrated the inauthenticity of belief and practices in modern economic institutions on a grand scale.[5] We refuse, he said, to abandon such towering myths as these: that the consumer controls the market with his purchases; that the government and the mature corporations are separate and distinct systems; that large firms oppose planning; that they do not necessarily seek maximum profits; that the Industrial System does not need the stimulation of vast expenditures for national defense; that economic growth is progress and is good for everyone; that the chief goal of the Industrial System is to serve man's needs. These are illusions at a high level; many others exist closer to the surface, like misleading advertising and huckstering over gadgets. These myths, according to Galbraith, plague socialist as well as capitalist societies.

Childhood Socialization and Authority Relations

Since the socialization of personality in the early years shapes the individual, it is a pivotal process in society. If authority relations are inauthentic, the estrangement is far less profound; if socialization is also affected, the split between societal appearances and reality is more likely to distort the human self.

Inauthentic socialization promotes self-images which are not committing or are in conflict. The youth may be trapped in a "double bind," a dilemma in which either of two actions will be the wrong one—he cannot win.[6] For example, the neurotic angry mother says, "Johnny, you know I love you, don't you?" While Johnny senses a contrasting emotion, stemming from a second set of signals mother is giving off, he cannot openly disagree for fear of his mother's response—and he wants to avoid telling a lie. Such a double bind not uncommonly leads to mental illness. The "social" counterpart should be clear, as if there are voices saying, "Johnny, you know everyone has an equal chance; you know the school is doing its best to encourage your individuality; you know the goal in life is to develop character, not to make a million dollars. . . ." Through such hazes the capacity for the authentic expression of emotions and feelings is inhibited. The school system has been accused of similar distortions, of preparing youth for a pseudo-*gemeinschaft* without encouraging authentic expressions of self.[7]

Criticism against the inauthenticity of mass culture, entertainment, and leisure activities is well-known.[8] This has been countered with the notion that it is an elitist intellectual projection and that the media reflect the desires and needs of the mass.[9] Future studies will have to determine (1) the extent to which mass culture materials can be upgraded in quality and still remain competitive; (2) the extent to which the acceptance of these popular materials is authentic (whether there are signs of rejection below the surface); and (3) the degree to which the acceptance of inauthentic culture results from inauthentic socialization, community, authority, and work, and the lack of continued exposure to more authentic culture.

Inauthenticity in the Affluent Society

The question is not whether this or that institution is inauthentic. The issue is *the quality of the whole society*. We suggest (1) that no group or society can lead an authentically rich and rewarding life amidst the deprivation of others; (2) that the more self-aware, educated, articulate, and mobilized members of the affluent society are clearly less (not more) committed to this affluent society than those less endowed. Possibly, the majority of the people have similar basic needs but are less aware of them and less able to express their disaffection; (3) the high rates of personal costs—neuroses and deviant and asocial behavior—suggest inauthenticity; and (4) no society that stresses material affluence can overcome the prevalence of the instrumental orientation among its members and, therefore, be authentic. A much greater focus on shared symbols and on a purposive orientation—a positive "mission in life"—is a prerequisite.

The affluent society may well be less alienating than early industrial society, but it is less authentic. Even if the affluent society is the most responsive in history, still it does not seem highly responsive.

Inauthentic societies are less responsive than *alienating* ones in two ways: (1) there are more limitations on the gathering of valid societal knowledge and collective self-consciousness because of the confusing haze, and, hence, on the mobilization of most members for political action; and (2) increasingly the identity of the citizen is built around the rejection of some foreign power and the maintenance, in non-war years, of a semi-military mobilization.

It may be said that an increase in societal responsiveness to allow for more authentic participation in shaping work, more adequate public services and facilities, decreased inequality, and so on will undermine the conditions of instrumentality and the utilitarian system and its Protestant Ethic. *In rejoinder,* one could propose that only a person who is authentically committed and gratified will be highly productive, as in the case of "pioneer" groups carving out a new and challenging frontier. But even if activation entails some sacrifice in the standard of living the citizens—if fully aware of the choices and options involved—may still opt for an active society. *Heightened activation* seems to be the best, perhaps the only, way to release the material and political and psychic energies necessary to reduce inequality, to transform ethnic and status relations, and to overcome tribalism and the wars that accompany it.

An active society would absorb the energies of its members, in particular their political energies. Societies lose this capacity for the utilization of energy as their institutions become more rigid and more instrumentally oriented. Even though their leaders want change, institutions tend to persevere as if they had a life of their own. All of this reduces the degree to which the members' energies are committed and their belief in the legitimacy of the institutional structure. If no mechanisms for activation and transformation are operative (or tolerated) and they are replaced with manipulation, inauthenticity will grow. This will increase the potential for radical and violent mobilization (Ku Klux Klan, Hell's Angels, Red Guard) which, in turn, becomes the mechanism for recommitment to a new and unknown, possibly regressive, set of institutions.

The Project, Again

A *project* is a concentrated act. It points to a relatively specific goal or goals. It stimulates a heightened level of activity, thus usually a measure of mobilization. It occupies a limited time period. While one project may lead to another or be combined with others into a more macroscopic one, an ongoing activity is not a project. Desegregation is a project; education is not. We introduced the project in Chapter 13; since it is crucial to social change, we return to it as our final topic.

Existentialist writings supply a background for the project notion. Man is viewed by existentialists as a self-transcending being, one who has a measure of choice (often exaggerated in this highly voluntarist philosophy); and his being is expressed in the choices he makes and in the projects he undertakes.[10] Thus man *pro-jects himself.*

An alienated man in existentialist writings is a man who does not make choices, who evades his responsibility; we would say, he is passive (not active), not engaged in his "own" projects. This may follow either because he has been reduced to an object, or because he is entangled in unresponsive projects—

those which involve treating others and himself as "things" and which prevent responsiveness to basic human needs.

PROJECTS AND AUTHENTIC PARTICIPATION

In an inauthentic society, the person faces the basic options of committing himself to a project or accepting passivity. While we reject the voluntaristic viewpoint of many existentialists, we believe that even the most oppressed person (e.g. the slave) has some measure of choice. Evidence shows that in most situations, outside authorities cannot fully commit a person's psychological, intellectual, and utilitarian resources; he retains the capacity to commit some of them, and, above all, some of himself, as he sees fit. What he sees as fit will be affected by his social context and may be distorted. But there are moments, we suggest, in which each man sees the roots of his unease, the shadows of his captors, and the hands of his manipulators. Thus he commands an irreducible element of freedom, small though it may be. *This freedom he can extend by committing himself to a project.*

Initially this may be limited—a small step toward some additional understanding of himself or social institutions or some minimal participation in events like signing a petition. This may increase, though at each step he may relapse into passivity (this is increasingly less likely as he collectivizes and organizes his projects and joins with like-minded others), or he may choose an inauthentic project.

Some projects are inauthentic in themselves, for example, a personal project that is materialistic and individualistic. A collectivistic-materialistic project entails the kind of objectivization commonly encountered in totalitarian production units. Both of these are closer to activeness, but both are inauthentic.

A personal project which is symbolic and related to a collective project, such as participation in a social movement, is more likely to be authentic than the kinds just described. Its goal may be the change of one of the two elements of the inauthentic condition (or various combinations thereof): (1) It may expose the facade, unveiling the underlying structure, thus increasing realistic societal knowledge and awareness, and foreshortening the distance between the private and public selves. This, in turn, makes more personal energy available for societal action. On the one hand, this is expected to promote a more authentic life, even if the existing structure does not yield; on the other hand, it is very difficult to initiate, advance, and sustain, unless it is supported by projects on other levels. (2) Such personal projects may lead to changes in the alienating structure itself, *if* they are linked to each other, and if they are collectivized and organized. It is extremely seldom that a Ralph Nader can affect institutions single-handed (and of course he received support once he had "broken the back" of the issue). In short, personal activation may lead only to new societal insight for the person, or it may lead to broader change.

FUNCTIONS OF PROJECTS

Most people are too entrenched in existing structure to initiate a symbolic-collective project; many are programmed by habit and respond robot-like to stimuli. Innovation is the role for a selected few. Once a project is under way, of course, legions may join. Given such support, macroscopic projects do several things. They provide a base for mobilization by freeing individuals from at least part of the guilt they experience in taking this "anti-social" step, release energy spent in self-defense, expose institutional flaws and rigidities thus allowing for more rational conduct, and serve as a basis for building counter-symbols and ideals as well as primary interpersonal relations to satisfy members' needs for recognition and affection—all without their having to conform to conventional norms.

Active groupings formed around a project face all the traps which can ensnare a personal project. Above all, it may be "individualistic," concerned with the grouping only, rather than with the society which contextuates it. The utopian communes—"islands"—popular with the New Left in the later 1960s, are a case in point.[11] Authenticity cannot be advanced in this way, for many reasons. The bases of political power, economic exchange, and mass communications reside in the society at large. Unless these can be transformed, they (1) invade the "islands" and undermine their authenticity; (2) prevent the creation of a foundation for a new society which requires a state of its own, a productive base, and communicative institutions—features unavailable to islands; and (3) the guilt of the island's inhabitants for those left at sea further distorts the situation. Vicarious participation works both ways: Just as the protest of the few does activate (if only a little) the spectator majority, so the continued inauthentic life of the many handcuffs the freedom of the few.[12]

Continuing Movements and Activation

From these varied kinds of projects, social movements rise whose aim is the transformation of society. If the project is broad-based and reaches a high level of activation, under favorable circumstances it may produce fundamental social change. Even when mobilization is modest and the alienating forces are too strong, inauthenticity still may decline because in the confrontation the underlying structure is unveiled. Its inauthenticity is made visible, to the actives and in some cases to members of elites themselves, who become prone to a "Damascus Road" kind of conversion. Thus followers of Senator McCarthy and their project in 1968 spotlighted the inauthenticity of the Vietnam war. (This principle holds not just for social movements seeking more responsive structures but also for those which seek the opposite, and not only for future-oriented ones but for past-oriented movements as well.)

Such projects, of course, often fail to achieve wide activation. Enthusiastic activeness may rise temporarily only to subside again, after either a victory, when members lose their drive, or a defeat, when spirits drop. To mold a permanent social-movement society, there must be the continued initiation of new societal projects which respond to increasingly more encompassing bases of membership and, as we shall see, to more symbolic and collective needs. These gains are not made in sudden, easy, and graceful jumps. The outcomes of one generation's projects require additional transformation by the next. *Authenticity can be maintained only by continued activation.* Ultimately, there is no end but rather a continuous drive toward realization. This is not a statement of despair, because each round of completed projects opens new and "higher" options, and the engagement in projects itself has an activating quality.

The relations between personal and social activation may be highlighted by the following point: Studies in several societies show that workers, asked if they wanted additional material goods, replied in the affirmative.[13] This may mean that it is "human nature" to wish for piles of consumer goods. A quite different interpretation, however, may be given the same data. The individual may be ambivalent, attracted both to material and individualistic rewards *and also* to symbolic and collectivistic ones. When this same individual is asked, for instance, if he favors the use of one half of one per cent of his tax money for raising the cultural level of his country, he might also reply in the affirmative. Thus, we submit, there may be as much of a personal foundation for a symbolic-collectivistic choice as there is for a materialistic one. This is especially true if the society has experienced success with earlier symbolic-collectivistic programs—they become a *fait accompli.* Witness the way in which West Europeans view social security and full employment as "inevitable."

Finally, societies, like groups and their combinations, have projects of their own. In the past, however, societies have been mobilized mainly to impose their wills on other societies or on their own dissident groups. Yet more positive projects are possible. Of special importance are guiding and mobilization *on the supranational level* (1) to prevent wars (and the preparation for wars) from draining societal energy, assets, and attention required for domestic projects, and (2) to gain resources with little societal strain by increasing the scale of the units of action, in conjunction with other nations.

Ultimately, a society's projects cannot be advanced unless they affect the societal boundaries. Contemporary reality is one of sub-global quasi-empires. The (almost utopian) *replacement of these with more egalitarian regional and world communities* is likely to entail projects in which units in "have not" societies will join with those in affluent nations. These pan-national projects seek the transformation of the whole system toward one which is more responsive internally and externally as well.

Projects act like catalysts, supporting each other up and down the micro-macro-ladder in a mutually reinforcing process. The individuals involved gain a more valid view of society, so that they can spur mobilization and the forces working to reduce alienation. Chain reactions are set in motion, which may go far beyond the initial action, like the sit-in by black college students at a Woolworth lunch counter in Greensboro, North Carolina, on February 2, 1960, ushered in an avalanche of such confrontations. Even when chain reactions "take off," however, they stall before the society is transformed, especially when organized resistance mounts. But rarely does the society remain the same after activation, because even if the chain of projects does not change the society's structure, the bases of mobilization are likely to have been affected, and new foundation has been set for future projects. Some groups disband after a failure; others, their members and their tools sharpened, prepare for another try. Sail on, sail on and on!

The Self-Guiding Society

Guided social change can be wrought in two ways. These two correspond roughly to the two major substantive parts of this volume: greater control (moving downward) and greater consensus (moving upward).

1. *Change can be propelled by elites.* Since this means the surrender of some power, it is uncommon in history. Yet elites still may make the decision, for three kinds of reasons.

Change may come with their emerging realization that greater consensus will move them, as well as the entire society, closer to survival, even to a more authentic society. It may be forced upon them by the rising mobilization of committed collectivities. And change will be speeded by the increasing symbolization of society, which gives intellectuals and professionals greater leverage over knowledge and decision-making. Social science knowledge, research, and criticism can contribute to all three courses.

2. *Change can be propelled by mobilized groups.* A main strand of modern history—since 1215—documents the process. When vast collectivities (e.g., minorities, youth, intellectuals, and professionals) become activated by organization, their potency can topple social walls. Before this moment, of course, patient groundwork is needed: research, case-building, criticism of elite policies, organization, leadership, the augmentation of consciousness in members, the mounting of projects, and the formation of alliances.

Any future is possible. This book has set forth a framework for analyzing the conditions under which man can change social institutions toward greater authenticity. With added consensus and equality, the society gains the capacity to exert greater contextuating controls over the units. Using these new powers of guidance, it can reset the social code and move to seek its goals and the goals of its members. If somehow a number of societies succeed in this quest, they may also be able to shift their boundaries, in the direction of a world society and an end to war.

NOTES

*Detailed references will be found in *The Active Society*, pp. 661–666).

1. Barbara W. Tuchman, *The Proud Tower* (New York: Macmillan, 1966), p. 165.

2. Melvin Seeman, "Alienation, Membership, and Political Knowledge," *Public Opinion Quarterly*, Vol. 30 (1966), pp. 353–367.

3. S. N. Eisenstadt, *Modernization: Protest and Change* (Englewood Cliffs: Prentice-Hall, 1966).

4. Reinhard Bendix, *Work and Authority in Industry* (New York: Wiley, 1956), pp. 308–318.

5. John Kenneth Galbraith, *The New Industrial State* (New York: Signet, 1968).

6. Gregory Bateson *et al.*, "Toward a Theory of Schizophrenia," *Behavioral Science*, Vol. 1 (1956), pp. 251–264.

7. Edgar Z. Friedenberg, *Coming of Age in America* (New York: Random House, 1965); Paul Goodman, *Growing up Absurd* (New York: Random House, 1956).

8. See Norman Jacobs (ed.), *Culture for the Millions* (Boston: Beacon, 1961).

9. Edward Shils, "Mass Society and its Culture," in *ibid.*, pp. 1–27.

10. William A. Luijpen, *Existential Phenomenology* (Pittsburgh: Duquesne University Press, 1963), pp. 279–281.

11. See, for example, B. F. Skinner, *Walden Two* (New York: Macmillan, 1961).

12. See the panel discussion by youth and their elders in Milton Mayer, *On Liberty: Man v. the State* (Santa Barbara: Center for the Study of Democratic Institutions, 1969), pp. 146–191.

13. Alex Inkeles *et al.*, *Becoming Modern* (Boston: Little Brown, 1959).

INDEX

INDEX

INDEX

INDEX